"The Death Coach: A Guide for Death Doulas Supporting Hospice Patients and Their Families"

Jocelyn D. Campbell

About the Author

Jocelyn Campbell, also known as *The Death Coach*, is a compassionate, empathetic, and dedicated hospice professional and hospice owner who is deeply committed to ensuring that all families have a good death. She recognizes that while hospice care is essential in providing comfort and support during the end-of-life journey, there are still gaps in the clinical care continuum that need to be addressed. Her background as a certified death doula gives her a unique perspective on the needs of hospice patients and their families. She understands the importance of providing emotional and practical support especially in the last weeks of life. She recognized that this support needed to be more extensive in traditional hospice care models. As she works with hospice patients and their families, she began to identify areas where hospice care could be improved and were partnering with a death doula could make a significant impact.

Jocelyn believes that by partnering with death doulas, hospice care could become more robust, efficient and provide higher patient and family satisfaction. She understands how death doulas could assist with a higher acuity of end-of-life planning, providing non-medical comfort measures, and offer bereavement support to families during the dying process and after the death of a loved one. Jocelyn advocates for integrating death doulas into hospice care. She has started to build partnerships with death doulas in her service areas. Jocelyn works closely with hospice staff to develop protocols for working with death doulas and educate them on this partnership's benefits. She also provides training to death doulas on the hospice care model and the role they could play in providing support to patients and families.

Jocelyn's efforts are paying off as the partnership between hospice and death doulas is becoming more prevalent and increasingly successful. Hospice patients and their families reported higher satisfaction with their end-of-life experience, and hospice staff said increased efficiency in their care delivery and operations. The hospice staff appreciated the death doulas' support, which allowed them to focus on their clinical responsibilities and provide higher-quality care. Her work demonstrates the value of integrating death doulas into hospice care. By advocating for the inclusion of death doulas, Jocelyn continues positively impacting the lives of hospice patients and their families. She helps to improve the quality of hospice care. Her efforts serve as a model for other hospice professionals looking to provide a higher level of support to patients and families during the end-of-life journey.

Acknowledgments

I would like to take a moment to acknowledge the importance of death in our lives. While death may be a difficult and uncomfortable topic, it is an essential part of the human experience. By acknowledging death and the impact it has on our lives, we can begin to remove the fear and confusion that often surrounds it.

I want to thank all the healthcare professionals who have dedicated their lives to end-of-life care ESPECIALLY my team at The Lighthouse Community Hospice. Your compassion, dedication, and commitment to improving the quality of life for terminally ill patients and their families is an inspiration to us all. I want to express our appreciation to the patients and families who have allowed us to be a part of their end-of-life journey. Your bravery and resilience in the face of difficult circumstances have touched our hearts and made us better advocates for improved end-of-life care.

I want to thank all the researchers and scholars who have dedicated their time and energy to improving our understanding of end-of-life care. Your contributions to the field have been invaluable and have helped to shape the direction of our work. Lastly, we want to acknowledge the importance of competent and compassionate medical professionals in the end-of-life care continuum. You play a critical role in ensuring that patients and their families have the opportunity for a good death. By having open and authentic conversations about end-of-life care, you help to provide comfort, support, and guidance during a difficult time.

Thank you to all who have contributed to the field of end-of-life care. Your efforts have made a significant impact on the lives of those in need, and we are grateful for your dedication and commitment to this vital aspect of human life.

Finally, thank you to my daughter who has had to endure all my philosophical and ideological end-of-life conversations her entire life.

Contents

The Death Coach: A Guide for Death Doulas Supporting Hospice Patients and Their Families

CHAPTER 1. Introduction

End-of-life care is a crucial aspect of healthcare, as it provides comfort and support to individuals facing life-limiting illnesses. This type of care acknowledges that death is a natural part of life and seeks to provide a dignified and peaceful end-of-life experience for the individual and their family. In recent years, a new type of healthcare professional has emerged to support individuals and their families during this challenging time - the death doula. Death doulas provide emotional and physical support to individuals and their families during the end-of-life journey. They offer comfort measures, assist with end-of-life planning, and provide bereavement support to those grieving the loss of a loved one.

This book, *The Death Coach: A Guide for Death doulas Supporting Hospice Patients and Their Families*, provides an in-depth look at the role of death doulas in hospice care and the skills and preparation required to become a successful death doula. It explores the benefits of death doula services and the legal and ethical considerations of death doula work. It provides tips for building a successful death doula practice.

By reading this book, death doulas will gain a deep understanding of the importance of end-of-life care, the role of death doulas in hospice care, and the skills and knowledge required to provide compassionate care to individuals and their families during a difficult time. With this knowledge, death doulas can positively impact the lives of hospice patients and their families and build a successful career in this rewarding field. Imagine a family whose elderly mother has been diagnosed with a life-limiting illness. The family is filled with fear and uncertainty about the future and how they will care for their mother during her final days. That's where a death doula steps in.

Death doulas, also known as end-of-life doulas, are trained individuals who provide emotional, practical, and spiritual support to individuals and their families during the end-of-life journey. As a death doula, your role is to provide comfort and support to individuals and their families during difficult times. Imagine a hospice patient who has been struggling with pain and discomfort. As their death doula, you understand the importance of providing comfort measures, such as positioning and relaxation techniques, to ease their discomfort. But you also know that your role goes beyond just physical comfort. You offer emotional support by simply being there to listen and provide a comforting presence. You offer practical support, such as assisting with bathing and grooming, and spiritual support by providing a safe space for reflection and contemplation.

You meet with the family, listens to their concerns, and provides comfort and support. You can also assist with end-of-life planning, such as creating an advance directive and discussing the individual's wishes for their care. Doulas also offer practical support, such as helping with bathing and grooming, and emotional support, by simply being there to listen and provide a comforting presence. The death doula can also offer spiritual support, by providing a safe space for the individual and their family to reflect on their life, their beliefs, and what they hope for their future. The death doula foundationally provides a sense of peace and comfort through this personalized approach, allowing the individual and their family to focus on what truly matters during this difficult time. This book, *The Death Coach: A Guide for Death doulas Supporting Hospice Patients and Their Families*, provides an in-depth look at the role of death doulas in hospice care and the skills and preparation required to become a successful death doula. It explores the benefits of death doula services and the legal and ethical considerations of death doula work. It provides tips for building a successful death doula practice.

By reading this book, you will also gain a deep understanding of the importance of end-of-life care, the role of death doulas in hospice care, and the skills and knowledge required to provide compassionate care to individuals and their families during difficult times. With this knowledge, death doulas can positively impact the lives of hospice patients and their families and build a successful career in this rewarding field. According to the National Hospice and Palliative Care Organization

(NHPCO), in 2020, an estimated 1.5 million people received hospice care in the United States. The need for end-of-life support has continued to grow as the ageing population in the United States increases. In 2020, it was estimated that there were over 46 million people aged 65 and older in the country, representing 14.5% of the total population. This number is expected to grow to over 98 million by 2060.

Studies have shown that individuals who receive hospice care have a better quality of life, experience less distress and depression, and are more satisfied with their care than those who do not receive hospice care. Additionally, hospice care has improved patient, and family satisfaction, reduced hospitalizations, and improved end-of-life experiences. With the growing need for hospice care, the role of death doulas has become increasingly important in providing emotional and practical support to individuals and their families during the end-of-life journey. Death doulas offer a unique approach to hospice care, focusing on the individual and their needs rather than simply treating their medical condition. This personalized approach to hospice care can help individuals and their families have a more peaceful and fulfilling end-of-life experience.

This book is a guide for death doulas who are interested in supporting hospice patients and their families. It provides an in-depth look at the role of death doulas in hospice care, the skills and preparation required to become a successful doula, and the benefits of this rewarding career. *The Death Coach: A Guide for Death Doulas Supporting Hospice Patients and Their Families* is a practical guide for their daily practice. This book provides an in-depth look at the role of death doulas in hospice care and the skills and preparation required to become a successful doula. It explores the benefits of death doula services and the legal and ethical considerations of death doula work. It provides tips for building a successful death doula practice. The concept of "a good death" has been a subject of discussion and reflection for centuries. It refers to the idea that individuals should be able to die peacefully, with dignity, and be surrounded by loved ones. However, in recent times, the COVID-19 pandemic has disrupted the end-of-life experience for many individuals and their families, making it difficult for them to achieve a good death. A good death is often defined as peaceful, comfortable, and dignified. It is a death that aligns with the individual's values and beliefs. It allows them to maintain control over their care and experience. A good death is characterized by a sense of closure, the ability to say goodbye to loved ones, and the assurance that one's affairs are in order.

One example of a good death can be seen in the story of Sarah, a 75-year-old woman diagnosed with terminal cancer. Sarah had always been an independent, strong-willed individual who cherished her autonomy and dignity. As her health deteriorated, she became increasingly concerned about her end-of-life experience and what that would mean for her family and loved ones. With the help of her death doula, Sarah was able to put together a comprehensive end-of-life plan that honored her values and beliefs. She wrote a living will, create a list of her final wishes, and made arrangements for her funeral and body disposition. She also took the time to write personal letters to her loved ones, expressing her love and gratitude for their support.

As her health declined, Sarah could remain in her home, surrounded by her family and close friends. Her death doula provided emotional and practical support, allowing her family to focus on being present with Sarah and spending quality time with her. With the help of hospice care, Sarah could remain comfortable and pain-free until her passing. Sarah's death was peaceful and dignified, providing her family with a sense of closure and peace. Her death doula was there every step of the way, providing support, guidance, and comfort during a difficult time for all involved. Sarah's death was a testament to the importance of end-of-life planning and death doulas' role in helping individuals and their families navigate this challenging time.

Death doulas play a crucial role in supporting individuals and their families during the end-of-life journey, especially in the current COVID era. They offer emotional, practical, and spiritual support to individuals and their families and contribute to a good death in several ways. They provide comfort and peace to the individual during their end-of-life journey. They offer comfort measures, such as massages or other forms of touch, and work closely with the individual to ensure that their needs are met. They also support the family, assisting with practical issues and offering emotional and spiritual support.

Death doulas help individuals, and their families navigate the end-of-life journey, especially in the current COVID era when many individuals cannot have their loved ones by their side. They provide support and guidance, ensuring that the individual and their family receive the best possible care and support during this difficult time.

Furthermore, death doulas contribute to a good death by advocating for the individual and their needs. They work closely with the hospice care team to ensure that the individual's wishes are being met and that their end-of-life experience is as peaceful and dignified as possible. Finally, death doulas contribute to a good death by embracing the hospice philosophy of care. This philosophy emphasizes comfort and support rather than cure and recognizes that everyone's end-of-life journey is unique. By adopting this philosophy, death doulas help individuals, and their families find peace and comfort during the end-of-life journey.

CHAPTER 2: Understanding Hospice Care

End-of-life care is a crucial aspect of healthcare, as it provides comfort and support to individuals facing life-limiting illnesses. Hospice care is a type of end-of-life care that focuses on improving the quality of life for individuals and their families during this difficult time. This care is provided in a hospice setting, such as a hospice facility or the individual's home. It is designed to address the physical, emotional, and spiritual needs of the individual and their family. Hospice care has evolved into a comprehensive approach to end-of-life care provided by an interdisciplinary team of healthcare professionals, including doctors, nurses, social workers, and spiritual care providers. Hospice care is a growing field in the United States, with an estimated 1.7 million individuals receiving hospice care each year. Hospice care has improved the quality of life for individuals and their families, providing comfort and support during difficult times.

This book, *The Death Coach: A Guide for Death Doulas Supporting Hospice Patients and Their Families*, provides an in-depth look at the role of death doulas in hospice care and the skills and preparation required to become a successful death doula. It explores the benefits of death doula services and the legal and ethical considerations of death doula work. It provides tips for building a successful death doula practice. By reading this book, death doulas will gain a deep understanding of the importance of end-of-life care, the role of death doulas in hospice care, and the skills and knowledge required to provide compassionate care to individuals and their families during difficult times. With this knowledge, death doulas can positively impact the lives of hospice patients and their families and build a successful career in this rewarding field.

The Interdisciplinary Team Approach in Hospice Care

One of the key aspects of hospice care is the interdisciplinary team (IDT) approach. The IDT comprises a group of healthcare professionals from various disciplines who work together to provide comprehensive care to hospice patients and their families. This team-based approach ensures that the individual and their family receive the care and support they need during this difficult time.

The IDT typically includes the following members:
1. Physician: The physician provides medical care and oversees the patient's care plan. They manage the patient's symptoms and coordinate with other members of the IDT to ensure the patient's needs are met.

2. Nurse: The nurse provides hands-on care and manages the patient's symptoms. They also coordinate with other members of the IDT to ensure the patient's care plan is followed.

3. Social Worker: The social worker provides emotional support and assists with practical issues, such as financial planning and making arrangements for after the patient's death.

4. Spiritual Care Provider: The spiritual care provider offers spiritual and emotional support to the patient and their family. They may also provide grief support after the patient's death.

5. Volunteer: The volunteer provides practical support, such as running errands or providing respite care for the family, and often this is how death doulas begin their professional journey

6. Bereavement Coordinator: The bereavement coordinator supports the family after the patient's death. They may offer grief counseling, support groups, and other resources to help the family through the grieving process.

Each member of the IDT plays a unique role in the patient's care, and they work together to ensure the patient's needs are met. For example, the nurse may manage the patient's symptoms and coordinate with the physician to adjust the patient's medication regimen. The social worker may assist the family with practical issues, such as arranging hospice services in the home. At the same time, the spiritual care provider offers emotional and spiritual support.

The IDT approach provides a comprehensive approach to hospice care, ensuring that the patient and their family receive the care and support they need during this difficult time. As a death doula, it is important to understand the role of the IDT and how to work with each member to provide the best possible care to the patient and their family.

In conclusion, the interdisciplinary team approach in hospice care is crucial to providing comprehensive and compassionate care to individuals and their families during the end-of-life journey. The IDT works together to ensure that the patient's needs are met, and death doulas play an important role in supporting the IDT and providing comfort and support to the patient and their family.

Understanding the Hospice Philosophy of Care

The philosophy of hospice care is centered around the idea that everyone deserves a peaceful and dignified end-of-life experience. This approach to end-of-life care recognizes that death is a natural part of life and seeks to provide comfort and support to individuals and their families during this difficult time. The hospice philosophy of care emphasizes comfort and support rather than cure which means that hospice care focuses on managing symptoms rather than treating the underlying medical condition. Hospice care aims to improve the quality of life for the individual and their family rather than extending life.

This approach to end-of-life care is person-centered and tailored to the individual's unique needs and preferences. Hospice care is provided in a hospice setting, such as a hospice facility or the individual's home. It is designed to address the physical, emotional, and spiritual needs of the individual and their family.

The hospice philosophy of care recognizes that everyone's end-of-life journey is unique and seeks to provide care and support tailored to the individual's specific needs and preferences. This may include managing symptoms, providing emotional support, assisting with practical issues, and offering spiritual care. As a death doula, it is essential to understand the hospice philosophy of care and how it informs the approach to end-of-life care. By embracing the hospice philosophy of care, death doulas can provide compassionate and supportive care to individuals and their families during this difficult time. The hospice philosophy of care is centered around the idea that everyone deserves a peaceful and dignified end-of-life experience. This approach to end-of-life care recognizes that death is a natural part of life and seeks to provide comfort and support to individuals and their families during this difficult time. As a death doula, understanding the hospice philosophy of care is essential for providing compassionate and supportive care to individuals and their families during the end-of-life journey.

CHAPTER 3. The Role of Death Doulas in Hospice Care

Death doulas and end-of-life planners are unique professionals today as they play an important role in helping people prepare for the end of their lives. With a shifting consciousness around dying and a changing generational dynamic, the role of death doulas and end-of-life planners is becoming increasingly important. Today, people are starting to embrace a more conscious approach to death and dying; thus, normalizing the conversation, which means that individuals are beginning to view death as a natural part of life and are seeking ways to make the end-of-life experience more meaningful, dignified, and peaceful. Death doulas and end-of-life planners are well-positioned to help people navigate this process by providing emotional, practical, and spiritual support. One of the critical ways death doulas and end-of-life planners can contribute to this shift in consciousness is by encouraging individuals to examine their narratives on death and dying critically, which involves exploring cultural, philosophical, and personal perspectives on death and helping individuals understand how their beliefs and attitudes shape their end-of-life experience.

The aging population of the United States is growing at an unprecedented rate, with the number of adults aged 65 and older projected to nearly double from 52 million in 2018 to 95 million in 2060. This demographic shift has significant implications for the healthcare system, with older adults accounting for a disproportionate share of healthcare spending and an increased demand for end-of-life care. One of the challenges associated with this aging population is that many older adults still need to have children to serve as their primary caregivers. In fact, a significant number of older adults are becoming caregivers themselves, with nearly one in five grandparents serving as the primary caregiver for their grandchildren.

Despite this trend, children are still a significant source of care for older adults, with an estimated 43.5 million adults providing care for a family member or friend over the age of 50. Many of these caregivers are children who often juggle the demands of work, school and caring for a loved one. The burden of caregiving can be overwhelming for children. It can have a significant impact on their physical and emotional well-being. For example, studies have shown that children who serve as caregivers are at increased risk for depression, anxiety, and other mental health issues. Also, caregiving can interfere with their education and career goals, leading to long-term financial consequences.

As the aging population continues to grow, policymakers and healthcare providers must recognize the vital role that children play as caregivers and provide support and resources to help them meet the demands of caregiving. This may include providing education and training on caregiving techniques, connecting families with community resources, and offering financial assistance to help cover the costs of care. The aging population of the United States presents a significant challenge to the healthcare system, with many older adults relying on children as their primary caregivers. To ensure that these children can provide the care their loved ones need, it is vital to give them the support and resources needed to meet caregiving demands. The generational dynamic is also changing in today's society, as younger generations are viewing death and dying differently. They are more open to alternative approaches to end-of-life care, such as hospice and palliative care. They are more interested in finding ways to make the end-of-life experience meaningful and fulfilling. Death doulas and end-of-life planners can help these individuals by providing guidance, support, and practical tools for navigating the end-of-life journey.

In a hospice care setting, death doulas work alongside the interdisciplinary team (IDT) to provide comprehensive care to the individual and their family. They offer a supportive presence and provide emotional and physical comfort to the patient. Death doulas also offer support to the family, assisting with practical issues, such as making arrangements for after the patient's death and offering emotional and spiritual support. One of the critical responsibilities of death doulas in a hospice care setting is to provide comfort measures to the patient. This may include providing a calm and peaceful environment, offering massages or other forms of touch, and helping the patient to maintain their dignity and comfort. Death doulas may also support the family, assisting with practical issues and offering emotional and spiritual support.

In addition to providing comfort and support, death doulas play an essential role in communication and collaboration with the IDT. They work closely with other team members, such as the nurse and physician, to ensure that the patient's needs are met, and the care plan is followed. They may also assist the family with navigating the hospice care system and advocating for their loved one's needs. Some of the end-of-life services a death doula might offer includes:

- Companionship
- Hands-on, non-medical comfort measures
- Referrals to physical modalities, such as massage, reiki, acupuncture
- Bedside Vigil
- Household Support
- Logistical planning
- Life review, the meaning of life, legacy work
- Sacred Space
- Respite Care
- Spirituality
- Identification of community resources
- Patient Advocacy
- Advanced care planning
- Bereavement Care and Counseling
- Arrangements for dependent care or pet care
- Music thanatology

As a death doula, it is crucial to understand the role you play in the hospice care setting and how to work with the IDT to provide the best possible care to the individual and their family. By embracing the hospice philosophy of care and working alongside the IDT, death doulas can make a meaningful difference in the lives of individuals and their families during the end-of-life journey. The role of death doulas in end-of-life care has been growing in popularity, and for a good reason. Death doulas provide emotional, practical, and spiritual support to individuals and their families during the end-of-life journey. When partnered with hospice care providers, they can offer significant value-added benefits to the hospice and the individual.

Death doulas provide additional support to the individual and their family. They work closely with the hospice care team to ensure that the individual's needs are met and that their end-of-life experience is as peaceful and dignified as possible. This support can be precious when the individual's family cannot be present, as death doulas can provide the comfort and support the family would typically offer. Additionally, death doulas help to ease the burden on the hospice care team. They provide support and guidance to the family, freeing up time and resources for the hospice care team to focus on the individual's medical needs. This partnership allows the hospice care team to provide more comprehensive care to the individual, resulting in a better end-of-life experience. Thirdly, death doulas bring a unique perspective to the hospice care team. They are trained to focus on the individual's emotional, practical, and spiritual needs. They can offer insights and recommendations that the hospice care team may have yet to consider. This partnership can result in a more holistic approach to end-of-life care, which can lead to a more peaceful and dignified end-of-life experience for the individual. Finally, death doulas can help improve the family's bereavement process. They offer support and guidance to the family during the end-of-life journey and after the individual has passed away. This support can help the family process their grief and find peace, improving their overall well-being.

The partnership between death doulas and hospice care providers can bring significant value-added benefits to the hospice and the individual. Death doulas provide additional support to the individual and their family, ease the burden on the hospice care team, bring a unique perspective to the hospice care team, and help improve the family's bereavement process. By partnering with hospice care providers, death doulas can help to ensure that individuals have a peaceful and dignified end-of-life experience. By understanding the hospice philosophy of care and the role of death doulas in a hospice care setting, death doulas can make a meaningful difference in the lives of individuals and their families during the end-of-life journey.

There was a family with a mother diagnosed with a life-limiting illness. The family initially chose hospice care for their mother, as they wanted to ensure that she received the best possible care and support during her end-of-life journey. However, they soon realized that their mother had non-traditional death care wishes and that the hospice care she was receiving was not meeting all her needs. The family struggled to support their mother's non-traditional death care wishes, as they felt overwhelmed and unsure how best to care for her. They knew that they needed additional support, but they were not sure where to turn. That was until they heard about death doulas and the exceptional support they could offer. The family decided to engage the services of a death doula, and they were amazed at the difference it made. The death doula provided emotional, practical, and spiritual support to their mother, and she was able to provide comfort and peace during her end-of-life journey.

The death doula also worked closely with the hospice care team to ensure their mother's non-traditional death care wishes were met. The death doula also supported the family, assisting with practical issues, such as making arrangements for after their mother's death and offering emotional and spiritual support. The family felt grateful for the support they received from the death doula and thought it was instrumental in helping their mother have a peaceful and dignified end-of-life experience. This family's story highlights the importance of end-of-life care and death doulas' role in supporting individuals and their families during the end-of-life journey. By choosing to engage the services of a death doula, the family could ensure that their mother received the best possible care and support, even with her non-traditional death care wishes. The family was grateful for the support they received from the death doula and felt that it was instrumental in helping their mother have a peaceful and dignified end-of-life experience.

Chapter 4. Preparing for the Role of a Death Doula

Becoming a death doula requires providing emotional, practical, and spiritual support to individuals and their families during the end-of-life journey. To be effective in this role, death doulas must prepare themselves both physically and mentally for the challenges that they may face.

Education and Certifications

There are several education and certification programs available for death doulas. These programs range from online courses to in-person workshops. They typically cover end-of-life care, communication skills, and bereavement support. Although these programs are not required in every state, they can provide death doulas with a deeper understanding of the end-of-life process and the skills necessary to provide adequate support. Here is a list of some of the education and certification programs available for death doulas:

1. International End of Life Doula Association (INELDA) – INELDA offers a comprehensive training program for death doulas, including online courses and in-person workshops.

2. The National End of Life Doula Alliance (NEDA) – NEDA offers a certification program for death doulas, including online courses and in-person workshops.

3. The Conscious Dying Institute – The Conscious Dying Institute offers a certification program for death doulas, including online courses and in-person workshops.

4. The End-of-Life Doula Training Program – The organization "Doulagivers" offers this program. It gives death doulas the skills and knowledge necessary to provide effective end-of-life care.

5. The Association for Death Education and Counseling (ADEC) – ADEC offers a certification program for death doulas, including online courses and in-person workshops.

6. The International Association of Thanatologists – The International Association of Thanatologists offers a certification program for death doulas, including online courses and in-person workshops.

7. The National Hospice and Palliative Care Organization (NHPCO) – NHPCO offers training programs for death doulas, including online courses and in-person workshops.

8. Going with Grace offers a comprehensive training program for death doulas, including online courses and in-person workshops.

As outlined by the National End-of-Life Doula Alliance, the core competencies for death doulas include communication and interpersonal skills, professionalism, technical knowledge, values, and ethics.
- Death doulas must be effective advocates for the patient and their families. They must

communicate effectively with the patient and their wider circle of family and friends. They must also be able to facilitate family issues and help families say goodbye to their loved ones.

- Death doulas must protect themselves in their practice, be familiar with the Institute of Medicine's "Dying in America" report, know the Patient Bill of Rights and HIPAA requirements, and be committed to ongoing professional education and development.
- Death doulas must be knowledgeable about trends and specialties in end-of-life care, understand medical protocols and the natural death process, and be able to prepare and manage care plans for families and caregivers.
- Death doulas must set professional boundaries, maintain personal boundaries, develop core ethical qualities, and respect legal parameters.

Death doulas must possess communication and interpersonal skills, professionalism, technical knowledge, and values and ethics to provide high-quality end-of-life care to patients and their families. These are just a few education and certification programs available for death doulas. It is vital to research the different programs and choose the one that best fits your needs and goals. It is also important to note that while these certifications and training programs can provide valuable information and skills, they may only be required in some states.

Criminal Background Checks

Working with hospices often requires death doulas to undergo criminal background checks. These checks are designed to ensure the safety of hospice patients and their families and that death doulas have a clean criminal record. Death doulas should be prepared to undergo a criminal background check and to provide any necessary documentation, such as a fingerprint or background check form. In the United States, background checks are a standard requirement for hospice professionals to ensure the safety of patients and their families. The federal and state governments regulate the background check requirements for hospice professionals, including doulas. These requirements vary depending on the state where the professional will be working.

The federal government requires that all hospice professionals undergo a background check as part of the certification process. This check typically includes a review of the individual's criminal history and a check of the national sex offender registry. The background check is designed to identify any past criminal behavior that may pose a risk to patients and their families. In addition to federal requirements, each state has background check requirements for hospice professionals. Some states require additional background checks, such as fingerprinting or reviewing the state's criminal records database. Some states also have specific requirements for individuals living outside of the state or living in another country.

Hospice professionals must be aware of the background check requirements in their state, as failure to comply with these requirements can result in disciplinary action or even loss of certification. Hospice professionals should also be prepared to provide documentation and other information as required by the background check process. Overall, the background check requirements for hospice professionals in the United States are designed to ensure the safety and well-being of hospice patients and their families. These requirements are an essential part of the hospice care process, and hospice professionals should be familiar with the requirements in their state to ensure they are in compliance with all regulations.

Professional Tools

As death doulas embark on their journey of providing comprehensive end-of-life support, it is essential for them to continuously develop their offerings and define their mission which can be achieved through doula training and education programs that are designed to equip them with the skills, knowledge, and resources needed to provide the highest level of care to those they serve.

During doula training, death doulas can refine their skills and develop a deeper understanding of their role in end-of-life care. They will learn about the various aspects of hospice care and the multiple techniques and approaches that can provide comfort and support to individuals and their families. This includes understanding the hospice philosophy of care, the interdisciplinary team approach, and the role of death doulas in a hospice care setting. Additionally, doula training programs will allow death doulas to develop their interpersonal and communication skills, which are critical in providing compassionate and empathetic care to individuals and their families as they navigate their end-of-life journey. Death doulas will learn how to actively listen, communicate effectively, and facilitate family issues in a respectful and supportive way.

As they refine their skills through doula training, death doulas will define their mission and develop their service offerings, which includes determining the type of services they want to provide, the target audience they want to serve, and the areas of expertise they want to focus on. They may also explore different marketing strategies to help them reach their target audience and build a successful death doula practice. Doula training provides death doulas with the tools and resources needed to provide comprehensive end-of-life support to individuals and their families. Through this training, death doulas will refine their skills, develop a deeper understanding of their role, and define their mission, as they strive to make a positive impact in the lives of those they serve.

Planning for the Living While Waiting for Death

Planning for living is a crucial aspect of end-of-life care. It involves creating a comprehensive plan for one's end-of-life, which encompasses not just medical care but also personal, financial, and emotional considerations for the family the person will leave behind. Death doulas and end-of-life planners play a unique role in helping individuals and their families navigate this process, providing guidance, support, and resources.

Advance directives, living wills, and other legal documents are critical aspects of end-of-life planning. These documents outline the individual's wishes regarding medical treatment and provide guidance for healthcare providers and family members in the event of an emergency. Death doulas and end-of-life planners help individuals navigate the process of creating and updating these documents, ensuring that they are legally binding and reflect the individual's wishes.

Legacy projects, life reviews, and digital legacy arrangements are essential for end-of-life planning. These activities allow individuals to reflect on their lives and share their stories with loved ones. Death doulas and end-of-life planners can provide support and resources to help individuals create meaningful legacy projects, such as writing a memoir, creating a photo album, or preserving their digital legacy.

Funeral and body disposition methods are other vital aspects of end-of-life planning. Death doulas and end-of-life planners can help individuals understand the options available and make informed decisions that align with their beliefs, values, and budget. Whether it's a traditional funeral, cremation, or a home funeral, the death doula or end-of-life planner can provide guidance and support to help ensure that the individual's end-of-life wishes are honored.

In addition to these practical considerations, end-of-life planning involves cataloging possessions and financial information. Death doulas and end-of-life planners can help individuals create an inventory of their possessions and financial assets, ensuring that these items are distributed according to their wishes and that their families are not left with the burden of sorting through their belongings.

Finally, end-of-life planning also ensures that dependents and pets are taken care of after an individual's death. Death doulas and end-of-life planners can help individuals create a plan to maintain their dependents and pets, providing peace of mind that their loved ones will be taken care of. In conclusion, planning for the living is a critical aspect of end-of-life care. Death doulas and end-of-life planners play a unique role in helping individuals and their families navigate this process. By providing guidance, support, and resources, these professionals help ensure that individuals can make informed decisions, that their end-of-life wishes are honored, and that their families are not left with the burden of sorting through their belongings.

The Good Death: Planning for the dying

Death doulas provide outstanding and compassionate end-of-life support for individuals and their families. They offer a holistic approach that not only addresses the physical needs of the dying person, but also their emotional, spiritual, and practical needs. One of the critical roles of a death doula is to provide companionship and sitting vigil, which means being present with the individual during their final days and offering comfort, support, and a listening ear. The doula can also assist with caregiver respite, giving family members and loved ones a break from their caregiving duties and helping them to rest and recharge.

In addition to companionship, death doulas can assist with body disposition arrangements, including making arrangements for cremation, burial, or other forms of body disposition and ensuring that the individual's wishes are respected. The doula can also help with obituary and eulogy writing, offering guidance and support to the individual's loved ones as they write a tribute to their life.

Death doulas can also provide guidance and support for traditional and home funerals, including assisting with planning and preparing the funeral or memorial service and giving advice on the rituals and ceremonies appropriate for the individual's beliefs and cultural background. Finally, death doulas can also provide resources and support for individuals and their families as they navigate the end-of-life journey, including information on advance directives, funeral planning, financial and legal considerations, and grief support. With their comprehensive approach to end-of-life care, death doulas play a critical role in helping individuals and their families find peace and comfort during this difficult time.

Bereavement and Ancillary Support Services

The death of a loved one can be a traumatic and overwhelming experience, leaving behind a long list of tasks that need to be taken care of. In this time of grief, it can be challenging to focus on practical matters and handle the responsibilities that come with death which is where a death doula can offer invaluable support. After the death of a loved one, a death doula can help wrap up affairs and take care of essential tasks such as closing accounts, canceling services and utilities, handling and processing mail, and locating passwords for online accounts. These tasks can be time-consuming and emotionally taxing. Still, a death doula can help simplify the process and ensure that everything is taken care of in a timely and organized manner.

In addition to practical support, death doulas can also offer grief support to loved ones and families. They are trained to help individuals navigate the grieving process and can provide resources and referrals to support groups, counseling services, and other forms of help.

Finally, death doulas can help with the disposition of possessions and belongings. They can assist with organizing and distributing personal items, creating a plan for donating or selling things, and ensuring that the individual's belongings are handled with care and respect. Death doulas play a vital role in offering comprehensive support to individuals and families after death. Their practical and emotional support can help ease the burden of grief and ensure that the end-of-life process is handled with care and dignity.

Becoming a death doula requires providing emotional, practical, and spiritual support to individuals and their families during the end-of-life journey. To be effective in this role, death doulas must prepare themselves both physically and mentally for the challenges that they may face. This preparation can include education and certification programs, criminal background checks, and access to professional tools. By preparing themselves in these ways, death doulas can provide the best possible support to individuals and their families during the end-of-life journey.

Chapter 5. Developing Your Skills as a Death Doula

Determining the Components of End-of-Life Care you will Provide Services for

According to the National Hospice and Palliative Care Organization (NHPCO), in 2019, approximately 1.5 million people received hospice care in the United States. An estimated 60% of all deaths in the country occurred in hospice or palliative care settings. These statistics highlight the importance of hospice and palliative care in providing comfort and support to individuals and their families during the end-of-life journey. Hospice still needs to be utilized. Cultural and societal bias is one of the contributing factors. As a death doula, it is essential to understand and confront your privilege and biases. As you embark on this journey, you must be aware of your beliefs, values, and attitudes towards death and dying and how they may impact your work with patients and families.

One crucial aspect of confronting your privilege and biases is acknowledging your cultural background and how it influences your perception of death care. You may have grown up with beliefs about death and dying that may not be shared by the individuals and families you serve. Understanding this can help you to be more culturally competent and empathetic in your work. Understanding the systemic barriers and challenges that marginalized communities face in accessing quality end-of-life care is essential, which includes recognizing the impact of racism, classism, ableism, and other forms of oppression on individuals and families who are facing life-limiting illnesses.

By acknowledging these challenges, you can work towards creating a more inclusive and equitable deathcare system. Finally, it is essential to continuously educate yourself and stay informed about the latest developments in death care and end-of-life support, which includes participating in ongoing training and professional development opportunities, seeking out diverse perspectives, and engaging in open and honest conversations with colleagues, patients, and families. By confronting your privilege and biases and continuously educating yourself, you can become a more effective and compassionate death doula better equipped to support individuals and families as they navigate the end-of-life journey. Also, as a death doula, it is vital to understand your beliefs, biases, and structures surrounding death and dying. This self-reflection and evaluation will benefit not only the individuals and families you serve but also your personal growth and professional development.

One aspect of this self-reflection is understanding the privilege and bias in your belief systems. For example, as a death doula, it is essential to be aware of the cultural, socioeconomic, and historical differences that shape the end-of-life experiences of different communities, particularly communities of color and marginalized populations. To effectively support individuals and families from diverse backgrounds, seeking education and training on these issues is essential, including workshops and seminars, reading books and articles, and engaging in discussions with individuals from diverse communities. Additionally, it is necessary to be open to feedback and to work to challenge your own biases and beliefs actively, which may involve seeking out diverse perspectives and being willing to listen and learn from others. It is also essential to be aware of your cultural background and experiences' impact on your perceptions and attitudes towards death and dying.

You can become a more informed, compassionate, and effective death doula by confronting your privilege and bias. This self-reflection and growth will benefit the individuals and families you serve and your personal and professional development. Moreover, as someone who will die one day, it is essential to be mindful of your beliefs and attitudes towards death and dying. This self-reflection can provide valuable insights into your end-of-life preferences and help you better understand the perspectives of others. In conclusion, as a death doula, it is crucial to understand your beliefs, biases, and structures surrounding death and dying. By actively seeking out education and training, being open to feedback, and confronting your own privilege and prejudice, you can become a more informed, compassionate, and effective death doula, both personally and professionally.

Best Practices for Death Doulas

There are several best practices for death doulas, including maintaining open and effective communication with the hospice interdisciplinary team, providing compassionate and non-judgmental support to the individual and their family, and always maintaining a professional demeanor. As a death doula, providing compassionate and effective care to patients and their families during the end-of-life journey is crucial to your role. There are several best practices that you can follow to ensure that you are providing the highest quality of care possible.

1. Active Listening: One of the essential best practices for death doulas is active listening which means genuinely hearing and understanding what the patient and their family members are saying and being present in the moment with them.

2. Communication: Effective communication is critical for death doulas; it includes communicating clearly with the patient, their family, and healthcare providers and understanding and interpreting their needs and concerns.

3. Respect for Patient and Family Wishes: It is essential to respect the patient's and family's wishes and provide care that aligns with their values and belief. This may involve honoring cultural traditions or providing spiritual support.

4. Comfort and Pain Management: An essential aspect of end-of-life care is ensuring that the patient is comfortable and free from pain. Death doulas can work with healthcare providers to implement a medical and non-medical pain management plan. They can also provide emotional and spiritual support to help the patient and their family cope with the physical and emotional discomfort that may arise.

5. Emotional Support: Death doulas are critical in providing emotional support to patients and their

families during the end-of-life journey. This can include offering a listening ear, providing comfort and reassurance, and helping families to find closure.

6. Coordination of Care: Death doulas can help coordinate care between healthcare providers and other interdisciplinary team members. This includes ensuring everyone is on the same page and meeting the patient's needs and wishes.

7. Preparation for Death: Death doulas can help patients and their families prepare by guiding advance directives, funeral planning, and other end-of-life decisions.

Examples of each of these best practices in action:

1. Active Listening: A death doula may sit with a patient and listen to their story, taking the time to understand their experiences and provide comfort and support.

2. Communication: A death doula may help a patient's family communicate with healthcare providers and other interdisciplinary team members, making sure that everyone is informed and involved in the patient's care.

3. Respect for Patient and Family Wishes: A death doula may help a patient's family to arrange a traditional funeral or ceremony that honors their cultural beliefs and values.

4. Comfort and Pain Management: A death doula may provide comfort measures such as a hand to hold or a soothing voice. They may also work with healthcare

providers to manage the patient's pain through medication or other means.

5. Emotional Support: A death doula may offer a shoulder to cry on and comfort a patient's family as they navigate the end-of-life journey.

6. Coordination of Care: A death doula may help coordinate the care provided by healthcare providers and other interdisciplinary team members, ensuring that everyone is working together to meet the patient's needs.

7. Preparation for Death: A death doula may help a patient and their family to prepare for death by assisting with funeral planning and other end-of-life decisions.

Following these best practices, death doulas can provide comprehensive and compassionate end-of-life care to patients and their families. As a death doula, it is vital to regularly assess your effectiveness in supporting the patient and their family, which helps you improve your skills and ensure that the patient and their family are receiving the best possible care.

Some questions a death doula can ask to assess their effectiveness include:

1. How has my presence impacted the patient and their family?

2. Can I provide the emotional, practical, and spiritual support that the patient and their family need?

3. Can I provide comfort and peace to the patient and their family?
4. Have I been able to help the patient and their family navigate the end-of-life process in a way that is meaningful to them?

5. Can I help the patient and their family find closure and peace?
6. Can I effectively communicate with the patient's healthcare team and other involved parties to ensure that the patient's needs are being met?

7. Can I provide the patient and their family with the resources they need to cope with the end-of-life process?

8. Can I provide the patient and their family with dignity and respect during the end-of-life process?

By asking these questions and evaluating the answers, a death doula can assess their effectiveness in providing care to the patient and their family. This information can then be used to make changes and improve how the death doula provides care, ensuring that the patient and their family receive the best possible support during the end-of-life journey.

Understanding and Preventing Burnout in the Death Care Industry

As a death doula or any professional in the end-of-life care industry, it is essential to understand and recognize burnout symptoms, which can be physically and emotionally demanding. It is important to prioritize self-care to prevent burnout.

Symptoms of burnout include:
- Fatigue
- Physical and emotional exhaustion
- Decreased motivation and inspiration
- Feelings of cynicism and detachment
- Decreased job satisfaction
- Difficulty sleeping and concentrating

To prevent burnout, it is essential to prioritize self-care and seek support from colleagues and loved ones which can include:
- Taking breaks and vacations
- Engaging in physical activity or hobbies
- Seeking support from a therapist or support group
- Practicing mindfulness and stress-reduction techniques
- Maintaining a healthy work-life balance

It is also essential to seek support from colleagues and loved ones. The death care industry can be a close-knit community. It is necessary to foster relationships and support one another to prevent burnout. Additionally, it is required to have open and honest discussions with hospice and other care providers about workload and responsibilities, to avoid excessive stress and burnout. In conclusion, burnout is a common issue in the death care industry. Still, it can be prevented with proper self-care and support from colleagues and loved ones. It is important to prioritize self-care and seek help to provide the highest quality care for patients and their families.

Taking Care of Yourself: Self-Care for End-of-Life Professionals

As an end-of-life professional, you provide comfort, support, and guidance to individuals and families facing the end of life. It is a challenging and rewarding field, but it can also be emotionally and physically taxing. That's why self-care is essential for end-of-life professionals. This chapter will explore the importance of self-care, strategies for avoiding burnout, and tips for maintaining a healthy balance in your personal and professional life.

Why Self-Care is Important

End-of-life work can be emotionally demanding and taking care of yourself is essential to continue to provide the best possible care to others. Self-care can help you maintain your well-being and avoid burnout, which can negatively impact your work and personal life. Additionally, self-care can help you to stay motivated, focused, and energized so that you can continue to make a positive impact on the lives of those you serve.

Strategies for Avoiding Burnout

End-of-life work can be emotionally challenging, and it is essential to take steps to avoid burnout. Some strategies for preventing burnout include:
> • Prioritizing self-care: Make time for activities that you enjoy and that helps you to recharge, such as exercise, meditation, or hobbies.

• Building a support network: Surround yourself with friends, family, and colleagues who understand the demands of end-of-life work and can provide support and encouragement when needed.

• Setting boundaries: Be clear about what you can and cannot do, and don't be afraid to say "no" when you need to.

• Seeking professional help: If you are feeling overwhelmed, consider seeking the help of a therapist or counselor who can help you to manage your stress and emotions.

Tips for Maintaining a Healthy Balance

To maintain a healthy balance in your personal and professional life, it is essential to:

• Make time for yourself: Set aside time each day or each week for self-care activities that help you to recharge.

• Prioritize self-care activities: Make self-care a priority, and don't let other responsibilities get in the way.

• Stay connected with loved ones: Stay connected with friends, family, and loved ones, and make time for them in your schedule.

• Seek support when you need it: Don't be afraid to ask for help when you need it, whether from friends, family, or colleagues.

• Remember why you do what you do: Stay connected to your passion and purpose and remind yourself why you do what you do.

Self-care is essential for end-of-life professionals. It is important to prioritize it to avoid burnout and maintain a healthy balance in your personal and professional life. By taking care of yourself, you can continue to provide the best possible care to others and positively impact the lives of those you serve.

Chapter 6. Working with Clients and Their Families: Providing Comfort and Support

Comfort Measures for Hospice Patients

End-of-life care is a crucial aspect of healthcare, and comfort measures play a significant role in providing comfort and support to individuals facing life-limiting illnesses. As a death doula, your part is to provide comfort and support to individuals and their families during difficult times. One of the most important ways to do this is by using comfort measures. Comfort measures can take many forms, including massage, aromatherapy, and guided imagery. These measures can help to reduce anxiety and provide comfort during the end-of-life journey. They can also help individuals manage pain and other symptoms and promote a sense of peace and calm.

A massage is a form of touch therapy that can help to reduce pain and discomfort. It can also help to improve sleep, increase relaxation, and reduce stress and anxiety. Aromatherapy involves the use of essential oils to promote peace and well-being. Guided imagery visualizes peaceful and calming scenes, such as a beach or a forest, to help reduce anxiety and promote relaxation. In this chapter, we will explore how death doulas can use these comfort measures to provide support and comfort to hospice patients. We will also share the story of Lacy, a death doula who used these comfort measures to support a terminal Alzheimer's patient.

Lacy was a death doula who was called to support a terminal Alzheimer's patient. The patient suffered from pain and anxiety, and her family struggled to manage her care. Lacy met with the patient and her family to assess their needs and to create a care plan. She recognized that the patient was struggling with anxiety and pain and decided to use massage, aromatherapy, and guided imagery to help reduce these symptoms. Lacy began by using massage to help reduce the patient's pain. She used gentle, soothing touch to help relieve the patient's discomfort. Lacy also used aromatherapy, diffusing essential oils in the room to create a peaceful and calming atmosphere. Finally, she used guided imagery to help the patient visualize soothing scenes, such as a beach or a forest.

The patient's family was amazed at the difference these comfort measures made. They noticed a significant reduction in the patient's pain and anxiety, and they were able to provide more effective care. The patient could also sleep better and experience a greater sense of peace and comfort. Lacy's use of comfort measures was a testament to the importance of end-of-life care and death doulas' role in providing comfort and support to hospice patients. By using massage, aromatherapy, and guided imagery, Lacy could give the patient a more peaceful and fulfilling end-of-life experience.

Comfort measures play a crucial role in end-of-life care. Death doulas can use massage, aromatherapy, and guided imagery to provide comfort and support to hospice patients. Doing so can help reduce anxiety and pain, promote relaxation, and give a sense of peace and comfort during the end-of-life journey.

Supporting the Emotional Needs of Hospice Patients and Their Families

The end-of-life journey can be difficult and emotional for hospice patients and their loved ones. Hospice patients often experience feelings of fear, anxiety, and loneliness. In contrast, their families may experience sadness, guilt, and grief, which is where death doulas can play a critical role in providing emotional support to individuals and their families during this difficult time.

Death doulas are trained to provide emotional and spiritual support to individuals and their families during the end-of-life journey. They are non-medical professionals who offer a compassionate and empathetic presence, helping individuals and their families navigate the end-of-life journey with dignity and grace.

Sharon, a death doula, was engaged by the Williams family after his terminal diagnosis of John. John's wife and young children were having extreme difficulty caregiving and coping while John was dying. Sharon immediately recognized the emotional turmoil that the family was experiencing and knew that she needed to act fast to provide support. Sharon's priority was to provide a safe and comforting space for the family. She listened to their concerns and fears, offering comfort and reassurance. Sharon also helped the family to understand the grieving process and what they could expect in the coming weeks. Sharon also provided practical support to the family, allowing them to navigate the complex healthcare system and assisting with the logistics of end-of-life planning. She worked closely with John's medical team to ensure his wishes were being honored and that he received the best care.

In addition to providing practical support, Sharon also provided emotional support to John's wife and children. She offered a listening ear, provided comfort and support, and helped the family to process their feelings of sadness and grief. Sharon recognized that the family needed time to grieve and gave them the space and support they needed. Sharon's efforts made a huge difference in the lives of the Williams family. John was able to die peacefully and with dignity, surrounded by his loved ones. His wife and children were able to find comfort and solace in Sharon's support, and they were better able to cope with their loss.

Death doulas play a critical role in supporting the emotional needs of hospice patients and their families. They provide a compassionate and empathetic presence, helping individuals and their families navigate the end-of-life journey with dignity and grace. With their training, knowledge, and experience, death doulas can positively impact the lives of hospice patients and their families, helping them find peace and comfort during a difficult time.

Understanding the Grieving Process and Providing Bereavement Support

As a death doula, it is essential to understand the grieving process and the various stages that individuals and their families may experience after losing a loved one which includes recognizing the signs and symptoms of grief, as well as being able to offer bereavement support to individuals and their families during this difficult time. The grieving process is a unique and personal experience, and there is no right or wrong way to grieve. However, some typical stages that individuals may experience include shock, denial, anger, bargaining, depression, and acceptance. It is essential to recognize that these stages are not linear and that individuals may experience them in any order, or they may not experience them at all. As a death doula, it is vital to recognize the signs of grief and offer support and comfort to individuals and their families during this difficult time which may include listening to the individual's thoughts and feelings, offering a comforting touch, or simply being there for the individual as they work through their grief. You may also be called upon to help with funeral planning and the disposition of personal items, which can be a difficult and overwhelming task for individuals and their families, and death doulas can offer practical support and guidance.

Another example of Sharon's engagement included providing emotional support to John's wife and children, helping them to process their grief and navigate this difficult time. Sharon also helped the family with funeral planning and the disposition of John's items. She provided practical support, such as making arrangements with the funeral home and assisting with the closure of John's business matters. Sharon's compassionate and supportive approach helped the Williams family find some peace and comfort during this difficult time, and her support positively impacted their grieving process. Top of Form
Bottom of Form

Chapter 7. Preparing for End-of-Life Care working with a Hospice

COMMUNICATION AND INTERPERSONAL SKILLS

As a death doula, you play a critical role in advocating for the patient, their family, and the end-of-life doula (EOLD) profession. Your role as an advocate involves working closely with the patient, their family, and the healthcare team to ensure that the patient's priorities, healthcare treatment decisions, and spiritual goals are respected and honored throughout the end-of-life journey.

Advocating for Patient Priorities

One of a death doula's critical responsibilities is advocating for the patient's priorities. This may involve ensuring the patient's end-of-life wishes are respected and honored by the healthcare team. It may also include supporting the patient's comfort and well-being, ensuring they receive the best care during their final days. To effectively advocate for the patient, it is essential to understand their priorities and end-of-life wishes. This may involve having open and honest conversations with the patient and their family and reviewing any advance directives or end-of-life plans that have been put in place. By understanding the patient's priorities, you can work closely with the healthcare team to ensure they are honored and respected throughout the end-of-life journey.

Advocating for Healthcare Treatment Decisions

Another important aspect of advocating for the patient is ensuring that the patient's healthcare treatment decisions are respected. This may involve supporting specific treatments, such as pain management or symptom control, or ensuring that the patient receives the best possible care for their condition. To effectively advocate for the patient's healthcare treatment decisions, it is essential to understand the patient's medical condition and the available treatments. This may involve working closely with the healthcare team, reviewing medical records, and staying informed about the latest treatments and advancements in hospice care. By being knowledgeable about the patient's condition and available treatments, you can effectively advocate for them and ensure their healthcare treatment decisions are respected and honored.

Advocating for Spiritual Goals

It is crucial to advocate for the patient's spiritual goals. This may involve ensuring that the patient's spiritual beliefs and practices are respected and honored during the end-of-life journey. It may also include working with the patient and their family to provide spiritual support and guidance and to facilitate any spiritual rituals or practices that are important to the patient. To effectively advocate for the patient's spiritual goals, it is essential to understand their beliefs and practices and to be knowledgeable about different spiritual traditions and rituals. This may involve having open and honest conversations with the patient and their family and working closely with any spiritual leaders or practitioners involved in the patient's care. By understanding the patient's spiritual beliefs and practices and knowing about different spiritual traditions, you can effectively advocate for the patient's spiritual goals and provide support and guidance during the end-of-life journey.

The role of a death doula as an advocate is critical. It requires a deep understanding of the patient's priorities, healthcare treatment decisions, and spiritual goals. By working closely with the patient, their family, and the healthcare team, death doulas can ensure that their end-of-life wishes are honored and respected and that they receive the best possible care during their final days.

Example: Sharon, the Death Doula Sharon, was a death doula engaged by the Williams family after his terminal diagnosis of John. John was a loving husband and father of two young children, and his family struggled to care for him and cope.

Communicating with the individual's and families' wider circles

As a death doula, it is essential to understand that a hospice patient's end-of-life journey affects not only them but also their family and friends. Effective communication with a patient's wider circle of support is crucial in providing the best possible care and support during this difficult time.

One of the tools that death doulas can use to communicate with a patient's wider circle is a paper calendar or folder. This is a great way to keep track of important dates, appointments, and tasks related to the patient's care. The calendar or folder can also store important documents, such as advance directives or medical information. This way, everyone involved in the patient's care has access to the same information, making it easier to coordinate care and ensure that the patient's wishes are honored. Another tool that death doulas can use to communicate with a patient's wider circle is a care-share interactive website. These websites provide a platform for families and friends to access patient care information, including updates on their condition, events calendars, message and well-wisher boards, and tools for organizing events or photo galleries. This website can be beneficial for families who live far away and cannot visit the patient regularly.

In addition to these tools, death doulas can also assist families in setting up a timeline of events, such as doctor's appointments, medication schedules, and any other important dates related to the patient's care. This can help families keep track of what is happening and ensure everyone is on the same page. The role of a death doula is to provide compassionate and knowledgeable support to individuals and their families during the end-of-life journey. By using these tools and techniques to communicate with a patient's wider circle, death doulas can ensure that everyone involved in the patient's care is informed and up to date, making the end-of-life journey a little easier for everyone involved. An example of this type of communication in practice can be seen in the case of Karen, a death doula working with the Smith family. The family engaged Karen after their father, John, was diagnosed with a terminal illness. The Smith family was struggling with the demands of caregiving and coping with John's condition, and Karen was there to provide support.

One of the first things Karen did was set up a care-share website for the Smith family, which provided updates on John's condition, a calendar of events, and a message board for friends and family to leave well wishes. Karen also helped the family create a timeline of events, including doctor's appointments and medication schedules, to keep everyone informed and on the same page. Through her efforts to communicate effectively with John's wider circle of support, Karen provided a sense of peace and comfort to the Smith family. They felt that they were not alone in their journey and had a support system in place. Karen's advocacy and communication skills positively impacted the lives of the Smith family, and they felt grateful for the support they received during this difficult time. Death doulas are essential in advocating for patients, their families, and the end-of-life doula profession. By using practical communication tools and techniques, death doulas can provide support and comfort to individuals and their families during the end-of-life journey, making the experience a little easier for everyone involved.

Communicating effectively and actively listening

Communicating effectively is a vital aspect of the role of a death doula. It requires a combination of active listening, critical thinking, and creative problem-solving to build relationships with individuals, families, and healthcare teams. By being an effective communicator, death doulas can better understand the needs of their patients and families and provide the support they need.

Active listening is the foundation of effective communication. As a death doula, listening to what individuals and families say and understanding their perspectives is crucial. This means being present now, paying attention to non-verbal cues, and being empathetic. By actively listening to individuals and families, death doulas can better understand their needs and concerns and provide the support they need.

Critical thinking is also an essential aspect of effective communication. Death doulas must be able to analyze and evaluate information, consider alternative perspectives, and make informed decisions. This is particularly important in the context of end-of-life care, where there are often complex and challenging decisions to be made. By using critical thinking, death doulas can help individuals and families navigate these decisions and make informed choices about their care.

Creative problem-solving is a crucial component of effective communication. Death doulas must be able to think outside the box and find innovative solutions to the challenges they face. This may involve working with individuals and families to find new ways of coping with the end-of-life journey or exploring alternative treatment options to manage symptoms. By using creative problem-solving, death doulas can help individuals and families find peace and comfort during this difficult time.

Effective communication is a critical aspect of the death doula role. By combining active listening, critical thinking, and creative problem-solving, death doulas can provide the support individuals, and families need during the end-of-life journey. Through effective communication, death doulas can positively impact the lives of those they serve and build meaningful relationships with their patients and families.

Facilitating family issues

End-of-life care is difficult for individuals and their families, and it is not uncommon for families to experience discord during this time. As a neutral party, the death doula plays a crucial role in facilitating family issues and helping families navigate this difficult time. In this chapter, we will explore the techniques for dealing with family dissonance, identifying patterns in family dynamics, and knowing when to refer to specialists.

One of the most important tasks of a death doula is to help the patient and their family get their affairs in order, which can be a complex and emotional process. Still, ensuring that the individual's wishes are honored and that their end-of-life journey is as peaceful as possible is essential. The death doula can help by accurately communicating what is meant by "getting one's affairs in order," assisting the patient and family members in saying goodbye and facilitating closure.

It is common for family members to have different opinions and beliefs about the individual's end-of-life care. As a death doula, it is essential to have the skills and knowledge to deal with family dissonance, which may involve active listening, critical thinking, and creative problem-solving to help families reach a resolution that is in the patient's best interests.

The death doula must also be aware of patterns in family dynamics, such as power imbalances or past conflicts, and be able to address these issues sensitively and effectively. In some cases, it may be necessary to refer the family to a specialist, such as a counselor or a mediator, to help resolve any issues.

Finally, death doulas must understand the grieving process and be able to provide bereavement support to individuals and their families, which may include helping the family with funeral planning, offering support with the disposition of personal items, and facilitating the closure of business matters during the bereavement period. An example of a death doula who successfully facilitated family issues is Sharon, with whom the Williams family engaged after the terminal diagnosis of John. John's wife and young children were having extreme difficulty caregiving and coping while John was dying. Sharon was able to listen to the family's concerns and help them communicate effectively with each other. She also guided how to get their affairs in order and assisted the family in saying goodbye to John. Sharon's compassionate and practical approach helped the Williams family navigate this difficult time and find peace and closure.

Facilitating family issues is an essential aspect of death doula work. By using active listening, critical thinking, and creative problem-solving, death doulas can help families navigate the end-of-life journey and ensure that the patient's wishes are honored. Through their compassion and expertise, death doulas can make a positive impact on the lives of hospice patients and their families and help families find peace and closure during this difficult time the patient and family members in saying goodbye

In the final stage of life, individuals and their families must have vital paperwork to ensure their wishes and priorities are respected. As a death doula, knowing the various forms necessary to put these plans in place is crucial. This chapter will overview the key documents commonly used in end-of-life planning.

State-Specific Advance Directive Forms

Advance directives are legal documents that outline an individual's preferences for medical treatment if they cannot make decisions for themselves. These documents can specify an individual's preferences for medical treatments, such as the use of life support and their wishes for end-of-life care. Death doulas need to be familiar with the specific advance directive forms required in their state.

DPOA for Healthcare

A Durable Power of Attorney for Healthcare (DPOA-HC) is a legal document allowing an individual to appoint someone to make decisions about their medical treatment if they cannot do so. This document is essential for individuals who want to ensure that their healthcare decisions are carried out according to their wishes. Death doulas should be familiar with the process for creating a DPOA-HC and should be able to assist individuals and their families in putting this document in place.

POLST Paradigm Forms

The Physician Orders for Life-Sustaining Treatment (POLST) paradigm is a program that provides individuals with the opportunity to create a set of medical orders that reflect their end-of-life preferences. These orders can specify an individual's preferences for medical treatments, such as the use of life support and their wishes for end-of-life care. Death doulas should be familiar with creating a POLST form and be able to assist individuals and their families in putting this document in place.

Planning paperwork is an essential aspect of end-of-life care. Death doulas should know the various forms necessary to implement end-of-life plans, including advance directives, DPOA-HC, and POLST forms. By helping individuals and their families navigate the paperwork process, death doulas can ensure that their wishes and priorities are respected during the end-of-life journey.

Collaborating with other care providers

As a death doula, it is essential to collaborate with other care providers to provide the best possible care for the individual and their family. Building strong communication channels with outside agencies and encouraging participation and cooperation with the team are vital to providing a seamless end-of-life experience. This chapter will explore the importance of collaborating with other care providers, including medical, hospice, hospital, care facility personnel, alternative health practitioners, town, city, county, and state government officials, funeral professionals, home funeral guides, clergy, and other community services.

Building Strong Channels of Communication with Outside Agencies

Building solid communication channels is one of the most critical aspects of collaborating with other care providers. This involves communicating the individual's needs, preferences, and goals to the care team and ensuring everyone is on the same page. Regular meetings, whether in person or over the phone, can help to foster communication and collaboration between the death doula, the individual and their family, and other care providers.

Encouraging Participation and Cooperation with the Team

Encouraging participation and cooperation from all care team members are essential for providing effective and compassionate care. Death doulas can facilitate this process by encouraging open communication, active listening, and creative problem-solving. They can also help foster collaboration by working with the care team to identify the individual's needs and goals and ensuring everyone is working towards the same end.

Responding Constructively and Effectively to Other People's Ideas and Input

To collaborate effectively with other care providers, responding constructively and effectively to other people's ideas and input is essential. This may involve considering different perspectives, offering alternative solutions, and working together to find the best possible outcome. Death doulas can also facilitate this process by providing support, guidance, and a neutral perspective and encouraging open communication and active listening.

Creating a community resource list can help death doulas collaborate effectively with other care providers. This list should include a variety of resources, including medical, hospice, hospital, care facility personnel, alternative health practitioners, town, city, county, and state government officials, funeral professionals, home funeral guides, clergy, and other community services. By having a comprehensive list of resources, death doulas can easily refer individuals and their families to the right resources and ensure they receive the best care during the end-of-life journey.

Collaborating with other care providers is essential for providing effective and compassionate end-of-life care. By building strong communication channels, encouraging participation and cooperation, responding constructively and effectively to other people's ideas and input, and creating a community resource list, death doulas can ensure that individuals and their families receive the best possible care during the end-of-life journey.

PROFESSIONALISM

Professionalism is a critical component of being a death doula, as it establishes trust with clients and their families and protects the doula from potential legal and financial issues. Here are some key aspects of professionalism that death doulas should be aware of:

      1. Liability protection: Death doulas should have liability insurance to protect themselves from potential lawsuits. This insurance can

help cover the costs of legal fees and any settlements or judgments in case of a lawsuit.

2. Written agreements and contracts: Written agreements and contracts are critical to establishing a professional relationship between the death doula and their client. These agreements clearly outline the services that will be provided, the fees, and any payment schedules.

3. Fees and payment schedules: Death doulas should clearly understand what services they can legally charge for and what services must be volunteered. This includes setting clear and reasonable fees for their services and having a payment schedule.

By following these best practices, death doulas can establish themselves as professional and trustworthy end-of-life care providers while protecting themselves from potential legal and financial issues. Death doulas must be familiar with the Institute of Medicine's Dying in America report, which provides comprehensive recommendations for improving end-of-life care in the United States. This report is a valuable resource for death doulas to understand the current state of hospice care and the challenges patients and families face.

- Death doulas must also be knowledgeable about the patient Bill of Rights, which outlines patients' rights in hospice care. This includes the right to receive care that is consistent with their values and beliefs, the right to be informed of their medical condition and treatment options, and the right to make decisions about their care.

- To maintain confidentiality and privacy, death doulas must be familiar with HIPAA regulations and understand the importance of protecting patient information. They must also follow recognized social media use guidelines and policies, avoiding the confidential sharing of information or patient stories without permission.

- The Hospice Medicare Conditions of Participation§ 418 is another vital resource for death doulas to understand. This outlines the requirements for hospice providers and the services they must offer to patients and families. Death doulas must be familiar with the definitions and terminology, reporting procedures, philosophy, and goals of hospice care to provide the best possible support to their patients and families.

Knowing the pertinent Hospice Medicare Conditions of Participation (CoP)§ 418 is critical to being a death doula in hospice care. The Hospice Medicare Benefit, established in 1982, provides reimbursement for hospice care services to individuals who are terminally ill and have elected to receive comfort-focused care rather than curative care. The Hospice Medicare CoP sets the standards for hospice organizations to participate in the Medicare program. Death doulas need to be familiar with these standards.

One of the most critical aspects of the Hospice Medicare CoP is its definition and terminology, which includes the description of hospice care, the eligibility criteria for hospice services, and the various services covered. This information is critical for death doulas to understand, as it helps them to understand the scope of their role in hospice care and how they fit into the larger hospice care team. Another critical aspect of the Hospice Medicare CoP is its reporting procedures and requirements. These procedures and conditions outline the steps that hospice organizations must take to report patient information, including the types of information that must be noted, the frequency of reporting, and the process for submitting reports. Death doulas should be familiar with these procedures and requirements, as they may be called upon to assist with the reporting process.

The hospice care philosophy and goals are also outlined in the Hospice Medicare CoP. These goals include providing comfort-focused care, maintaining the dignity and respect of the patient, and promoting choice and self-determination. Death doulas should be familiar with these goals and understand how they align with their values and beliefs about end-of-life care. The Hospice Medicare Benefit covers services are also outlined in the Hospice Medicare CoP. These services include medical, nursing, social work, chaplaincy, and bereavement support. Death doulas should be familiar with these services and understand how they can complement and enhance the care provided by the hospice interdisciplinary team.

Finally, the Hospice Medicare CoP guides how to handle an emergency in hospice care. This information is critical for death doulas, who may be called upon to assist with emergencies. The CoP also provides guidance on how death doulas fit into the current hospice model and their role in providing care to patients and families. In conclusion, understanding the Hospice Medicare Conditions of Participation§ 418 is essential for death doulas in hospice care. This information provides a foundation for their work. It helps them to understand the regulations and standards that govern hospice care. As a death doula, staying informed and up to date with the expectations, limitations, policies, and protocols of local hospitals, hospices, and care facilities is crucial. This will help ensure that you can provide the best possible end-of-life support to patients and their families.

In addition, it is essential to be aware of the legal requirements for unattended deaths. This may vary depending on the state or jurisdiction in which you practice, so it is crucial to familiarize yourself with the specific laws and regulations that apply. Ongoing professional education, development, and improvement are also critical components of being an effective death doula. This may involve attending workshops, conferences, or training programs and reading relevant books, articles, and other resources. Finally, recognizing and managing self-care is crucial to avoiding burnout and maintaining a healthy work-life balance as a death doula. This may involve regulating emotions and behaviors and being mindful of caregiver burnout signs, such as exhaustion, irritability, and hopelessness.

By following these best practices, death doulas can establish themselves as professional and trustworthy end-of-life care providers while also taking care of their well-being and avoiding burnout and death doulas can establish themselves as professional and reliable end-of-life care providers while also protecting themselves potential legal and financial issues. They can play a vital role in improving the quality of life for patients and families in hospice care.

TECHNICAL KNOWLEDGE

Knowing about trends and specialties in end-of-life care is essential for death doulas to stay current and provide the best possible care for their clients. There are several vital movements and models of care that death doulas should be familiar with, including:

- **The Good Death**: This movement promotes a peaceful, dignified, and meaningful end-of-life experience. It emphasizes the importance of individual choice and control and the need for compassionate care and support.

- **Death Positive Movement:** This movement seeks to change the cultural narrative around death and dying, promoting a more open and honest conversation about the end of life. It aims to reduce fear and stigma surrounding death and to empower individuals to make informed decisions about their end-of-life care.

- **Palliative Care:** This specialized field of medicine focuses on relieving symptoms, improving quality of life, and providing emotional and spiritual support to individuals facing serious or life-threatening illnesses. Palliative care can be provided at any stage of disease and alongside curative treatment.

- **Biopsychosocial Cultural Spiritual Model of Care**: This model of care recognizes that end-of-life care involves not just physical symptoms but also includes emotional, social, cultural, and spiritual needs. It views the person as a whole, considering their individual beliefs, values, and support systems, and tailors care accordingly.

The dying individual may want closure, to be pain and fear-free, and to have their affairs in order. They may also value self-determination, as opposed to the former paternalistic model. This self-determination may also extend to their end-of-life decisions, such as their preferred body disposition arrangements and funeral plans.

Families must understand their dynamics, coping mechanisms, and psychological issues surrounding terminal illness, death, and bereavement. Every family is unique and may have different needs, beliefs, and coping strategies. By being aware of these factors, a death doula can provide tailored support and guidance to each family. In addition to understanding the needs and desires of individuals and families, death doulas must also be familiar with medical protocols, including universal precautions and the natural death process. This knowledge will allow them to provide safe and practical support, while also being able to respond to any medical emergencies that may arise. In conclusion, by using their intuition and being knowledgeable about medical protocols and the desires of individuals and families, death doulas can provide comprehensive and compassionate support at the end of life.

In the final stages of life, a person may experience several physical, emotional, and spiritual changes. Death doulas need to recognize the signs and symptoms of approaching death and active dying to provide the best possible care and support for the individual and their family.

One of the first signs of approaching death is often a decline in physical function, such as decreased mobility, loss of appetite, and difficulty sleeping. Other common signs include increased confusion, disorientation, and changes in breathing patterns. As death approaches, the body begins to shut down, and the individual may become less responsive and more peaceful.

Voluntary Stopping of Eating and Drinking (VSED) is a choice some individuals make in the end-of-life process. It is passive euthanasia, where the individual stops eating and drinking to hasten the dying process. Death doulas should be familiar with this option and respect the individual's decision while providing emotional support and ensuring comfort.

In some states and countries, medically assisted death is an option for individuals facing unbearable suffering at the end of life. This refers to the medication prescribed by a physician to hasten death. Death doulas should be knowledgeable about the laws and regulations surrounding medically assisted death in their area and provide support and resources for individuals and families who choose this option. Death doulas need to understand the signs and symptoms of approaching death and active dying to give the best possible care and support for the individual and their family. Death doulas should also be familiar with various end-of-life options and respect the individual's decisions while providing emotional support and ensuring their comfort.

What the doula's role is, and isn't

As a death doula, it is essential to have a clear understanding of your role and responsibilities. A death doula provides comprehensive end-of-life support to the dying person and their community of support. The doula's role can vary greatly depending on the individual's needs, preferences, and the care setting in which they are receiving care. In this chapter, we will explore what a death doula's role is and isn't and how care can differ in various care settings.

The death doula's role is to provide comfort, support, and advocacy to the dying person and their family. A doula is not a medical professional and does not provide medical care or make medical decisions. Instead, the doula collaborates with the hospice interdisciplinary team to ensure that the patient's needs and wishes are met. The doula is also responsible for providing emotional support, creating a peaceful and comfortable environment, and helping the patient and their family navigate the end-of-life process.

Knowing How Care Differs in Various Care Settings

The care provided by a death doula can vary greatly depending on the care setting in which the patient is receiving care. In an independent living setting, the doula may provide more hands-on care, such as helping the patient with activities of daily living. In contrast, the doula may focus more on emotional support and advocacy in a hospice facility. The doula needs to understand the expectations, limitations, policies, and protocols of each care setting to ensure that they are providing the best possible care for their patients.

The doula may provide hands-on care and emotional support in an assisted living setting. In a skilled nursing facility, the doula may need to work more closely with the medical staff to ensure that the patient's needs are met. In all care settings, the doula's role is to provide comfort, support, and advocacy to the dying person and their family. A death doula plays an essential role in providing comprehensive end-of-life support to the dying person and their community of support. The doula needs to understand their roles and responsibilities and how care can differ in various settings. By doing so, the doula can provide the best possible care to their patients and help them navigate the end-of-life process with comfort, dignity, and peace.

Preparing and managing care plans for family/caregivers

The role of a death doula involves providing comprehensive end-of-life support for the dying and their community of support. One of the critical aspects of this support is preparing and managing care plans for the family and caregivers. This involves several important considerations and steps that the doula should be familiar with and be able to guide the family through.

Protocol for Initial Care Plan Meeting: The first step in preparing a care plan is to hold an initial meeting with the patient, family, and other healthcare team members. During this meeting, the doula should facilitate open and honest communication about the patient's needs, goals, and priorities. This will help to ensure that everyone is on the same page and that the care plan is tailored to meet the unique needs and wishes of the patient.

Goals and Patient Priorities: The doula should work closely with the patient and family to identify the patient's goals and priorities. This may include managing symptoms, maintaining the quality of life, and ensuring that the patient is comfortable and free from pain. The doula should also consider the patient's spiritual and emotional needs and physical needs when developing the care plan.

Expectations for Actions and Timetables: The care plan should clearly outline the expectations for actions and the timeline for each step in the process. This will help the family and caregivers to understand what needs to be done and when and will help to ensure that everyone is on the same page.

Decision-Making Processes: The doula should also be familiar with the decision-making processes involved in end-of-life care. This may include identifying a designated decision-maker, creating a durable power of attorney, and creating an advance directive. The doula should be able to guide the family through these processes and help them to make informed decisions about their loved one's care.

Stumbling Blocks and Developing Contingency Plans: Stumbling blocks and challenges may arise during the end-of-life journey. The doula should be prepared to anticipate these and develop contingency plans to address them. This may include managing symptoms, handling unexpected events, and dealing with changes in the patient's condition.

Structure, Schedule, and Gatekeeper Role: The care plan should also be structured and scheduled to meet the patient's and family's needs. The doula should serve as the gatekeeper, ensuring that everyone follows the care plan and that all aspects of the patient's care are managed seamlessly and effectively.

Goals of Care Plans: The care plan aims to ensure that the patient receives the best possible care and support during the end-of-life journey. The doula should work closely with the patient, family, and healthcare team to achieve this goal, providing compassionate and supportive care every step of the way.

CHAPTER 8. Comfort, dignity, choice, meaning, connection, and "dying well."

This chapter will delve into comfort, dignity, choice, meaning, connection, and "dying well" as essential factors in end-of-life care. Death doulas are crucial in ensuring that these factors are addressed, and that the dying individual and their family receive the support they need.

Comfort is a top priority for those approaching the end of life. This can be achieved through physical, emotional, and spiritual means. Physical comfort can be achieved through pain management and symptom control. In contrast, emotional comfort can be achieved through companionship and support. Spiritual comfort can be achieved through meaningful rituals or ceremonies, connecting with one's faith or spirituality, and feeling a sense of peace and closure.

Dignity is also a crucial component of end-of-life care. This includes ensuring that the individual's rights and choices are respected and treated with respect and compassion. This also includes ensuring that their physical and emotional needs are met, and they are free from discomfort and pain.

Choice is also important in end-of-life care. Death doulas can help individuals and their families understand the various options available, such as hospice care, palliative care, and medically assisted death. They can also assist with decision-making, ensuring that the individual's wishes are honored, and their choices are respected.

Meaning is another essential factor in end-of-life care. This can be achieved through legacy projects, life reviews, and connecting with loved ones. Death doulas can assist with these activities, helping individuals and their families create meaningful memories and connect with their loved ones.

Connection is also crucial in end-of-life care. This includes connecting with loved ones, nature, one's spirituality, or a higher power. Death doulas can assist with these connections, helping individuals and their families find comfort and meaning in their final days.

"Dying well" is a concept that encompasses all of these factors. It means that the individual can approach death with comfort, dignity, choice, meaning, and connection. Death doulas play a crucial role in ensuring that individuals can die well, helping them and their families find comfort, purpose, and peace in the final days of life.

In terms of doula practice, it is essential to understand the difference between support and doing. Death doulas provide support, not treatment, and should always respect the individual's choices and decisions. Cultural humility is also vital in death doula practice, as it involves understanding and respecting the cultural beliefs, values, and practices of those you serve.It is also essential for death doulas to be aware of the needs of special populations, such as those who are marginalized or underrepresented, and to provide culturally appropriate support. This includes understanding the unique needs of individuals from diverse cultural backgrounds, LGBTQIA+, and those with disabilities. By understanding the importance of comfort, dignity, choice, meaning, connection, and "dying well," death doulas can provide comprehensive and compassionate end-of-life care to individuals and their families.

What to do when there is spiritual discord

As death doulas, it is crucial to recognize that individuals and families may have different beliefs and spiritual practices regarding end-of-life care. When there is spiritual discord, it can be challenging for the doula to provide support and comfort to the patient and their family. However, there are several strategies that death doulas can use to address this issue.

One approach is to use guided imagery or visualization. This involves helping the patient and their family to create a peaceful and calming mental image, which can be a powerful tool for reducing stress and anxiety. This can be particularly useful for individuals struggling with fear or discomfort around their end-of-life experience.

Another strategy is to facilitate a living funeral or wake. This is a gathering of family and friends who come together to celebrate the patient's life and share memories, stories, and support. This can be a powerful way to bring people together and to help the patient and their family to find meaning and connection in their end-of-life experience. Respite care is another option that death doulas can provide to families and caregivers. This involves taking a break from caregiving responsibilities and allowing someone else to step in and provide support. This can be essential for families to recharge, reduce stress, and avoid burnout. When there is spiritual discord in hospice care, death doulas can play a crucial role in helping patients and their families to find comfort, dignity, and meaning in their end-of-life experience. Using strategies such as guided imagery or visualization, living funerals or wakes, and respite care, death doulas can help bring peace and comfort to patients and their families during this difficult time.

Offering bereavement follow-up

The grieving process can be complicated and overwhelming when a loved one passes away. As a death doula, it is essential to understand the bereavement process and offer follow-up support to families and caregivers. Offering bereavement follow-up can help ensure that families receive the care and support they need during this difficult time.

When offering bereavement follow-up, it is vital to look for signs that the grieving process is not going well. This can include prolonged sadness or depression, difficulty sleeping or eating, and an inability to return to normal activities. If you notice these signs, making a referral for grief counseling may be necessary.

Grief counseling can give families the support and tools to process their emotions and work through their grief. A qualified therapist can help families understand the bereavement process and offer practical coping strategies. In addition to offering bereavement follow-up, death doulas can provide respite care for families and caregivers. Respite care can allow families and caregivers to take a break from the demands of caregiving and recharge their batteries. This can be especially important during the bereavement period, when families and caregivers may feel incredibly overwhelmed and need support. By offering bereavement follow-up and respite care, death doulas can help ensure that families and caregivers receive the support they need during this difficult time. With the proper care and support, families can work through their grief and begin the process of healing.

Recognizing and reporting domestic violence/child/elder abuse

As a death doula, it is essential to be aware of and trained in recognizing signs of domestic violence, child abuse, and elder abuse. These forms of abuse can be present at any stage of life, including at the end of life. Identifying them and providing the appropriate support and referrals for those affected is crucial.

Domestic violence is a pattern of abusive behavior in any relationship used by one partner to gain or maintain power and control over the other. It can take many forms, including physical, emotional, sexual, or psychological abuse. At the end of life, abuse may become even more pronounced as the abuser becomes more vulnerable and reliant on their partner or caregiver.

Child abuse is any mistreatment of a child under 18, including physical, sexual, emotional, or neglect. Death doulas must be aware of the signs of child abuse, as they may encounter children caring for a dying parent or grandparent.

Elder abuse is any form of mistreatment of an older adult, including physical, emotional, sexual, financial, or neglect. The elderly population is a vulnerable population, and death doulas may encounter older adults who are experiencing abuse.

If a death doula suspects abuse, it is essential to report it to the appropriate authorities, such as the local police or social services. Additionally, a death doula can provide referrals to organizations that specialize in providing support and resources for abuse victims. Providing a safe and supportive environment for all individuals, including those experiencing abuse, is vital. Awareness and training in recognizing signs of domestic violence, child abuse, and elder abuse are crucial. Death doulas can prevent and address abuse in end-of-life care by providing a safe and supportive environment, referring individuals to the appropriate resources, and reporting abuse when necessary.

Knowing what post-death care entails

Death doulas must comprehensively understand the post-death care process to support families and loved ones during this time effectively. Post-death care involves the physical and emotional preparation of a deceased person's body and the grieving process of those left behind. One of the critical aspects of post-death care is knowing who may perform the care. In many cases, funeral directors and mortuary professionals are responsible for preparing the body and conducting necessary procedures. In other cases, families may choose to care for their loved one themselves or with the help of a death doula.

Another critical aspect of post-death care is understanding the conditions under which the care may be performed. For example, specific procedures may be restricted by law or cultural tradition. Additionally, there may be particular conditions surrounding the care of the body, such as the presence of a communicable disease or the need for an autopsy. Death doulas must be familiar with the post-death care process and the various players involved. This knowledge will help doulas to provide families with the support and resources they need during this challenging time and to ensure that their loved ones are treated with the dignity and respect they deserve.

VALUES AND ETHICS

In end-of-life care, it is vital for death doulas to set clear professional boundaries to provide the best care for their clients and protect themselves from potential legal and ethical issues. This chapter will explore the importance of establishing professional boundaries in the role of a death doula. The first step in setting professional boundaries is understanding the scope of practice and limitations of the doula role. Death doulas are not medical professionals and should not attempt to diagnose or treat medical conditions. They are trained to provide emotional, spiritual, and practical support to individuals and families during the end-of-life process. This means that they should not offer medical advice or interfere with the medical care provided by healthcare professionals.

In addition to understanding the limitations of their role, death doulas should also be familiar with the Code of Ethics that governs their practice. This code outlines the ethical principles and standards that death doulas should adhere to in their work, such as maintaining confidentiality, avoiding conflicts of interest, and providing compassionate and non-judgmental support.

Another important aspect of setting professional boundaries is maintaining professional behavior consistent with established ethical practices. This includes respecting clients' privacy, avoiding inappropriate relationships, and avoiding conflicts of interest. Death doulas should also be aware of the importance of self-care. They should take steps to regulate their emotions and behaviors to prevent burnout.

As a death doula, it is essential to maintain personal and professional boundaries to provide the best possible care for patients and their families. A death doula must possess core ethical qualities, including integrity, honesty, fairness, transparency, and accountability. They must also understand the doula model of care, which is non-medical, non-judgmental, and provides whole-person and whole-family care. One of the critical components of maintaining personal boundaries is self-awareness and insight into personal attributes and limitations. Death doulas must be aware of their own emotional and physical limitations and how they may impact their ability to provide care. They must also practice appropriate behavior for their role, representing themselves and the death doula profession.

It is also crucial for death doulas to be aware of and adhere to local, state, and federal laws as they pertain to healthcare and end-of-life care. This includes being knowledgeable about legal parameters and respecting the boundaries set by these laws. In addition to maintaining personal and professional boundaries, death doulas must also be committed to ongoing professional education, development, and improvement. They must stay up to date on best practices and trends in end-of-life care to provide the best possible support to patients and their families.

Maintaining personal and professional boundaries is essential for death doulas to provide the best care for patients and their families. By possessing core ethical qualities, understanding the doula model of care, and respecting legal parameters, death doulas can establish themselves as professional and trustworthy end-of-life care providers.

Chapter 9. Ethical and Legal Considerations in Hospice Care

The 'Good Death' by whose definition

As a death doula, it's essential to understand that the concept of a "good death" can vary significantly across different societal and cultural demographics. What may be considered a peaceful, dignified, and meaningful death for one person may be vastly different for another. Doulas must be culturally sensitive and aware of these differences to provide the best possible support for the dying person and their loved ones.

For example, a death doula named Sarah was working with a patient who was part of a Native American tribe. The patient had expressed a desire to be surrounded by their family and community members during their final moments. However, Sarah was unaware that it was essential to the patient's tribe to sing traditional songs and perform specific rituals during the dying process. Sarah learned about this through her patient's family members. She was able to incorporate these cultural practices into their end-of-life care plan.

This experience highlighted the importance of being culturally competent and aware of the patient's and family's specific needs and beliefs. Death doulas must be open-minded and willing to learn about different cultural practices, beliefs, and customs surrounding death and dying. It's also crucial for doulas to work closely with the interdisciplinary hospice team to ensure that the patient's cultural and societal beliefs are respected and incorporated into their care plan.

As a death doula, it's essential to understand that the concept of a "good death" can differ across different cultural and societal demographics. By being culturally sensitive and aware, doulas can provide personalized, respectful, and meaningful end-of-life care that honors the patient's beliefs and values.

Ethical Considerations for Death Doulas in Hospice Care

It is also essential to be aware of the ethical considerations that come with providing hospice care. To maintain the trust of the patient, their family, and the healthcare team, it is critical to adhere to a strict code of ethics. Here are some of the most important ethical considerations to keep in mind:

Confidentiality: Patients and their families often share sensitive and personal information with their death doula. It is crucial to maintain the confidentiality of this information and only share it with yourself if the patient or their legal representative gives permission. Death doulas should be familiar with HIPAA regulations and other privacy laws and ensure that all records and communications are confidential.

Conflicts of Interest: Death doulas should avoid any conflicts of interest arising during their work with a patient. For example, they should not have any financial relationships with the patient or their family or provide them with goods or services they would not offer to any other patient.

Compassionate and Non-Judgmental Support: Death doulas should provide compassionate and non-judgmental support to their patients and their families, regardless of their beliefs, values, or lifestyle choices. They should not impose their own beliefs or opinions on the patient and respect their right to make decisions about their end-of-life care.

Legislation: Several pieces of legislation address ethical considerations in hospice care, including the Patient Bill of Rights and the Hospice Medicare Conditions of Participation. Death doulas should be familiar with these laws and regulations and ensure that they are following them in their work.

To assess the effectiveness of a death doula in supporting a patient and their family, the following questions can be helpful:

1. How well does the death doula communicate with the patient and their family?
2. Does the death doula provide non-judgmental support and respect the patient's decisions?
3. Does the death doula maintain confidentiality and avoid conflicts of interest?
4. How well does the death doula collaborate with the healthcare team and other care providers?

5.   Does the death doula provide practical and emotional support to the patient and their family?

By answering these questions, the patient and their family can better understand the death doula's effectiveness in providing hospice care and make an informed decision about their end-of-life care.

Understanding Hospice Regulations and Laws

As a death doula, it is essential to understand the regulations and laws surrounding hospice care to provide the best support possible to patients and their families. Death doulas should be aware of several critical pieces of legislation, including the Health Insurance Portability and Accountability Act (HIPAA), the Patient Self-Determination Act, and the Hospice Medicare Benefit.

HIPAA regulations are designed to protect the privacy and security of individuals' health information. As a death doula, it is essential to understand these regulations and to ensure that all patient data is kept confidential and secure. This includes ensuring that any written or electronic records are stored securely, and that sensitive information is not shared with unauthorized individuals.

The Patient Self-Determination Act requires that healthcare facilities provide patients with information about their right to make decisions about their medical treatment, including end-of-life care. This means that patients have the right to decide about the type of care they receive and the treatments they receive. Death doulas should be familiar with these rights and how to support patients in making informed decisions.

The Hospice Medicare Benefit provides coverage for hospice care for individuals who are enrolled in Medicare. Death doulas should understand the requirements for Medicare coverage, including what types of care are covered and the conditions that must be met to receive this coverage. They should also be familiar with the different types of hospice care, including inpatient, respite, and home hospice care, and be able to help patients and their families navigate these options and make informed decisions.

Best Practices for Ethical and Legal Hospice Care

In addition to these regulations and laws, death doulas should also be aware of the ethical considerations in hospice care, including maintaining confidentiality, avoiding conflicts of interest, and providing compassionate and non-judgmental support. This includes avoiding situations where their personal beliefs or opinions may conflict with the wishes of the patient or family and ensuring that all interactions are respectful and supportive.

Death doulas must follow best practices for ethical and legal hospice care, including maintaining open and effective communication with the interdisciplinary team, avoiding conflicts of interest, and following all relevant regulations and laws. By understanding these regulations and laws and being mindful of the ethical considerations in hospice care, death doulas can provide the best possible support to patients and their families during the end-of-life journey.

Chapter 10. Exploring the Benefits of Death Doula Services

As death doulas, it is essential to be aware of the ethical considerations of providing care to those at the end of life. Many ethical dilemmas can arise in this work, and it is crucial to navigating these situations with compassion, integrity, and professionalism. One of the fundamental principles of ethical caregiving is confidentiality. This means that death doulas must respect the privacy of their patients and their families and not disclose any information that is shared with them in confidence. This can be particularly challenging when working with individuals at the end of life, as they may share sensitive information about their health, relationships, or finances.

Another important ethical consideration is avoiding conflicts of interest. Death doulas must be impartial and not influenced by personal beliefs or biases. They must also be mindful of their emotional well-being, as it is vital to maintain a level of detachment to provide adequate care. In addition to these ethical considerations, death doulas must also be aware of the relevant regulations and laws that govern hospice care. This includes HIPAA regulations, which dictate how patient information can be used and disclosed, and the Patient Self-Determination Act, which gives patients the right to make informed decisions about their care.

Ultimately, engaging in the ethics of caregiving requires a deep commitment to compassion and professionalism. Death doulas must balance their needs and beliefs with their patients and their family's needs and desires. By being mindful of these ethical considerations, death doulas can provide high-quality care that is both compassionate and respectful. One of the most important considerations is ensuring that the rights and privacy of the patient and their family are respected. This includes adhering to HIPAA regulations, which protect the confidentiality of patient health information. The Patient Self-Determination Act requires that hospice patients and their families be informed of their rights to make decisions about their healthcare, including the right to create an advance directive.

In addition to these regulations, death doulas must be aware of the Hospice Medicare Benefit, which provides coverage for those eligible for hospice care. It is essential to understand the requirements of this benefit and how it can be used to support the needs of the patient and their family. Another important aspect of ethical and legal hospice care is avoiding conflicts of interest. This includes ensuring that the death doula has no financial or personal interests that could interfere with its ability to provide impartial and compassionate support to the patient and their family. To maintain the highest standards of ethical and legal hospice care, death doulas should seek ongoing training and education to stay up to date on the latest regulations and best practices. This will help ensure they are equipped to provide the best possible support to those in need.

Death doulas must also be able to support their clients in creating a comprehensive end-of-life plan.

The following is an example of what most of these plans contain.

A Comprehensive End of Life Plan template may include the following key elements:
1. Personal Information:
- Name, Date of Birth, and Social Security Number
- Contact Information: Phone number, Email, and Physical Address
- Health Information: Primary Care Physician, Current Health Condition, and Health History
- Emergency Contact Information: Name, Relationship, and Contact Information

2. Advance Directives:
- Living Will: A document that outlines your preferences for medical treatment if you become unable to make decisions for yourself
- Durable Power of Attorney for Healthcare: A document that appoints someone to make decisions on your behalf if you become unable to make decisions for yourself
- Do Not Resuscitate Order (DNR): A document that instructs healthcare providers not to perform CPR if your heart stops or you stop breathing

3. Legacy Projects and Life Review:
- Personal History: Childhood memories, education, work experience, family history, and personal milestones
- Letters to Loved Ones: Letters to be shared with family and friends after your passing
- Personal Belongings: A list of personal belongings and instructions for their distribution

4. Digital Legacy:

- Online Accounts: A list of online accounts and passwords
- Digital Assets: A list of digital assets, including music and photos, and instructions for their distribution

5. Funeral and Body Disposition:
- Funeral Preference: A description of your preferred funeral or memorial service
- Body Disposition: A description of your preferred methods of body disposition, such as cremation or burial

6. Funeral Director: The name and contact information of the funeral director or funeral home you have selected

7. Possessions and Financial Cataloging:
- Possessions: A list of possessions and instructions for their distribution
- Financial Information: A list of bank accounts, investments, and other financial assets, along with instructions for their distribution

8. Dependent and Pet Care:
- Dependent Care: A description of the care you would like provided for dependents, such as children or elderly parents
- Pet Care: A description of the care you would like provided for pets, including their care and eventual disposition

9. Important Information and Documents:
- Legal Documents: A list of important legal documents, including wills, trusts, and powers of attorney
- Personal Records: A list of vital personal records, such as birth certificates and passport

It is essential to regularly update this comprehensive end-of-life plan as circumstances and preferences change. It is also necessary to ensure that a trusted individual is aware of its existence and has access to it in an emergency. By following these best practices for ethical and legal hospice care, death doulas can help ensure that the needs of the patient and their family are met with compassion, dignity, and respect and that the rights and privacy of all parties are protected.

Chapter 11. Building a Successful Death Doula Practice & Marketing Your Services as a Death Doula in Hospice Care

Networking with Hospice Organizations and Building Your Reputation

As a death doula, networking with hospice organizations and building your reputation within the community are crucial aspects of developing your practice and growing your client base. By establishing solid relationships with hospice organizations and demonstrating your expertise and compassion in end-of-life care, you can position yourself as a trusted resource for families and healthcare providers.

One of the key ways to build your reputation and network with hospice organizations is by volunteering or offering your services pro bono to hospice patients and families in need. This allows you to gain experience, demonstrate your skills, and build relationships with healthcare providers and other deathcare professionals. You can also attend conferences and workshops, join professional organizations, and participate in community events to connect with other death doulas, hospice providers, and funeral directors.

Another way to build your reputation is by providing excellent care to your clients and their families. This involves being knowledgeable, compassionate, responsive to their needs and taking the time to understand their unique end-of-life journey. You should also be able to communicate effectively with the interdisciplinary team, including doctors, nurses, social workers, and chaplains, to ensure that the patient's needs are being met.

In addition to building your reputation, you should also focus on marketing and promoting your services to reach potential clients and partners. This can include creating a website, brochures, and other marketing materials showcasing your experience, qualifications, and services. You can also use social media and other online platforms to reach a wider audience and connect with potential clients and partners. Ultimately, building your reputation and networking with hospice organizations will take time and effort. Still, demonstrating your expertise, compassion, and commitment to end-of-life care can establish you as a trusted and respected death doula in your community.

Finding Clients and Building Your Hospice Death Doula Practice

As a hospice death doula, building a solid client base is crucial to the success of your practice. Here are some strategies for finding clients and building your hospice death doula practice:

1. Networking: Attend local events and conferences related to hospice care and end-of-life support and join professional organizations in your area. This will allow you to connect with hospice organizations and healthcare professionals and showcase your expertise and services.

2. Building Relationships: Develop strong relationships with hospice organizations by offering your services

as a resource for their patients and families. Offer presentations or workshops on hospice care and end-of-life support and provide educational materials and resources to the organizations.

3. Online Presence: Build a solid online presence by creating a website and social media profiles that showcase your services and expertise. Be sure to include testimonials and reviews from past clients to build trust and credibility.

4. Referrals: Encourage current clients to refer friends and family members who may benefit from your services. Offer incentives for referrals, and make sure to thank your clients for their support.

5. Marketing Materials: Create marketing materials such as brochures, business cards, and flyers to promote your services and distribute them in your community and at local events and conferences.

6. Building Your Reputation: Provide exceptional care and support to your clients and their families and ask for feedback and testimonials to help build your reputation. Share your successes and positive feedback on social media and your website to showcase your expertise and dedication to your clients.

By following these strategies, you can build a successful hospice death doula practice that provides compassionate and professional support to those in need.

Several effective marketing strategies for death doulas in hospice care include speaking at industry events, participating in professional organizations, and leveraging social media. By combining these strategies, death doulas can build their reputation and reach a wider audience. The follows some effective marketing strategies for death doulas:

1. Networking: Building relationships with hospice organizations, healthcare providers, and other end-of-life professionals can help you get referrals and word-of-mouth recommendations. Attend industry conferences and events and reach out to local hospices to introduce yourself and your services.

2. Online Presence: Develop a robust online presence through a professional website and social media platforms. Your website should be user-friendly, visually appealing, and provide detailed information about your services. Utilize social media platforms like Facebook, Twitter, and LinkedIn to promote your services and engage with your target audience.

3. Content Marketing: Creating and sharing educational and informative content about end-of-life care and the role of a death doula can help build your reputation and attract potential clients. Write blog posts, create videos, and produce infographics to share on your website and social media platforms.

4. Direct Mail: Consider reaching out to potential clients through direct mail. Create a targeted

mailing list of people who have shown interest in end-of-life care or have been impacted by a loved one's death. Send them educational materials, brochures, and information about your services.

5. Community Outreach: Participate in community events and initiatives related to end-of-life care. Offer workshops, speak at local organizations, and provide educational materials to help raise awareness about your services.

6. Referral Marketing: Encourage existing clients to refer friends and family members who may benefit from your services. Offer incentives and rewards for successful referrals and thank your clients for their referrals.

Implementing these marketing strategies, death doulas can reach their target audience, build their reputation, and attract new clients in the hospice care industry. It's important to remember that marketing takes time and effort, but the long-term benefits are worth the investment.

The selling proposition for hospices

Adding a death doula to an Interdisciplinary hospice team (IDT) can significantly improve the end-of-life experience for patients and their families while providing several financial benefits for the hospice organization.

First, death doulas bring a unique and valuable set of skills to the IDT. They are trained in end-of-life care and specialize in providing emotional, spiritual, and practical support to patients and their families. This support can help alleviate the burden on other members of the IDT, such as nurses and social workers, who may be stretched thin with a high patient load. Death doulas can also help ensure that the patient's end-of-life experience is as peaceful and dignified as possible, leading to increased satisfaction among patients and their families.

Second, the presence of a death doula can help reduce costs associated with end-of-life care. A study published in the Journal of Palliative Medicine found that hospice patients who received doula care had shorter hospital stays and lower care costs than patients who did not receive doula care. This suggests that the presence of a death doula can help reduce the need for expensive medical interventions, such as hospitalization, and lead to more cost-effective care.

Third, adding a death doula can improve patient and family satisfaction with hospice care. Patients and families who receive end-of-life support from a death doula are more likely to rate their experience with hospice care as positive, which can lead to increased referrals and a more substantial reputation for the hospice organization.

Adding a death doula to a hospice IDT can provide a range of benefits, including increased support for patients and families, reduced costs of care, and improved patient and family satisfaction. These benefits make a case for the fiscal viability of adding a death doula to a hospice IDT and suggest that this investment can pay off in the long run.

The average cost of hospice care in the United States is typically determined based on several factors, including the type of hospice care provided (inpatient, outpatient, or routine home care), the specific services offered by the hospice, and the location of the hospice. For routine home care, the average cost per patient per day can range from $150 to $300 nationwide, depending on the specific services provided by the hospice and the location of the hospice.

The cost of services for a death doula can vary depending on several factors, such as location, experience level, and the specific services offered. On average, the cost of death doula services can range from $50 to $200 per hour. Some death doulas may offer packages that include several hours of support for a flat fee. It is important to note that death doula services are not typically covered by insurance, and individuals are responsible for paying for these services out of pocket. However, some hospices and palliative care organizations may offer death doula services as part of their overall care package. In this case, Medicare or other insurance plans may cover the cost. It is always best to discuss the cost of death doula services with the doula or their organization directly, as they can provide specific pricing information and answer any questions you may have.

Sometimes, families may pay for death doula services out of their funds or through community fundraising efforts. Despite the cost, many families find that the support and guidance provided by a death doula are invaluable, as it helps them navigate a difficult and emotional time with greater ease. The cost of death doula services is a small investment in ensuring that individuals and their families have a peaceful and dignified end-of-life experience. Adding a death doula to the hospice interdisciplinary team would increase the cost of hospice care. If the death doula is paid an hourly rate of $50 per hour, for example, and averages one hour per patient, the cost of the death doula would be $50 per patient per hour. the exact cost of adding a death doula to the hospice interdisciplinary team will depend on several factors, including the type of hospice care provided, the specific services offered by the death doula, and the location of the hospice. However, it is likely that the cost of adding a death doula to the hospice interdisciplinary team would be covered by the daily reimbursable rate by Medicare, Medicaid, or private insurance and would not significantly impact the overall cost of hospice care and patient satisfaction survey scores.

Chapter 12. Conclusion

The cost of death in America can vary greatly depending on several factors, such as the type of funeral or burial service, location, and individual preferences. On average, a traditional funeral with a casket and burial can cost anywhere from $7,000 to $10,000 or more. This cost includes embalming, body preparation, funeral director services, and the casket price and burial plot. Cremation is becoming a more popular and affordable alternative, with the average cost ranging from $2,000 to $4,000. This cost includes cremation, an urn for the ashes, and memorial services.

End-of-life expenses can also include costs for hospice care, medical treatment, and prescription drugs. These costs can add up quickly and be a financial burden for families already dealing with the emotional toll of a loved one's illness and death. Sometimes, life insurance policies, funeral trusts, or pre-arranged funeral plans can help cover these costs. However, many families still struggle to pay for these expenses and may need to turn to government programs, such as Medicaid, or seek financial assistance from charitable organizations. It is important to note that the cost of death in America is not just financial. The emotional and psychological toll on families and loved ones can be significant and long-lasting. Individuals need to plan for their end-of-life needs and consider the economic costs and emotional and psychological impact on those they leave behind. This is why the death doula industry is growing in leaps and bounds.

The role of a death doula extends beyond providing emotional and physical support to individuals and their families during the end-of-life journey. Doula services can also be used to support non-medical on-call needs in hospice care, providing a much-needed supplemental resource to the social worker, chaplain, and bereavement coordinator.

One area where death doulas can be particularly useful is in supporting "frequent flyer" patients who are at high risk for going to the emergency room. These patients often require additional support and attention, and the presence of a death doula can help to reduce their anxiety and provide comfort, reducing the likelihood of unnecessary hospitalization.

Death doulas can also provide support to the hospice outside of regular business hours, serving as an on-call resource for non-medical needs. For example, they can assist with providing information and support to families who are struggling to cope with the end-of-life journey of a loved one. They can also provide assistance with funeral planning, offer support with the disposition of personal items, and facilitate the closure of business matters during the bereavement period.

By partnering with or even hiring a death doula, hospice organizations can increase patient and family satisfaction and improve efficiency in hospice care delivery and operations. Doula services can provide much-needed support to the social worker, chaplain, and bereavement coordinator, allowing them to focus on other aspects of patient care. For example, Jocelyn Campbell, a hospice professional and certified death doula, noticed that many families were not receiving the support they needed during the end-of-life journey. She identified care gaps in the clinical care continuum and began exploring opportunities for how partnering with death doulas could improve patient and family satisfaction and increase efficiency in hospice care delivery and operations.

By partnering with death doulas, Jocelyn saw firsthand the positive impact they can have on the lives of hospice patients and their families. The death doulas provided emotional and physical support to individuals and their families, reducing the likelihood of unnecessary hospitalization, and improving overall patient and family satisfaction.

Summary of Key Points and Takeaways

As a death doula or end-of-life planner in hospice care, it is essential to understand your role in supporting patients and their families. The role of a death doula is multi-faceted. It encompasses a range of responsibilities, including companionship, caregiver respite, body disposition arrangements, obituary and eulogy writing, traditional and home funeral guidance, ritual or ceremony creation, and resources.

One of the key takeaways from this book is the importance of ongoing professional development and education. Death doulas should be familiar with the Institute of Medicine's Dying in America report, the Patient Bill of Rights, HIPAA regulations, the Patient Self-Determination Act, and the Hospice Medicare Benefit. In addition, death doulas should be committed to ongoing professional education and development and recognize the importance of self-care to avoid caregiver burnout.

Another important aspect of death doula work is awareness of ethical considerations in hospice care. Death doulas should maintain open and effective communication with the hospice interdisciplinary team, avoid conflicts of interest, and follow all relevant regulations and laws. It is also vital for death doulas to be aware of the ethical considerations in caregiving and engage in the ethics of caregiving.

Finally, as a death doula in hospice care, you must network with hospice organizations and build your reputation. This can be achieved through marketing strategies, such as creating a comprehensive end-of-life plan and finding clients.

Final Thoughts and Recommendations for Death doulas in Hospice Care

As a death doula in hospice care, it is vital to have a passion for helping others and a commitment to ongoing professional development and education. You should be familiar with the key regulations and laws, ethical considerations in hospice care, and the importance of self-care. It is also essential to have strong interpersonal skills, including active listening, critical thinking, and creative problem-solving. This will enable you to effectively communicate with patients, families, and other care providers and collaborate with them to provide the best possible end-of-life care.

Finally, it is essential to have a positive and compassionate attitude and a deep understanding of the value of a "good death." You should be committed to making a difference in the lives of hospice patients and their families and be prepared to offer comprehensive end-of-life support. Encouragement to Continue Making a Difference in the Lives of Hospice Patients and Their Families. As a death doula in hospice care, you can make a profound difference in the lives of patients and their families. Your role is critical in helping patients and families navigate the end-of-life journey, and you have the potential to provide comfort, support, and compassion at a time when it is needed most. We encourage you to continue working as a death doula in hospice care and making a difference in the lives of patients and their families. Your dedication and commitment to providing the best possible end-of-life care will have a lasting impact, and we are confident that you will continue to make a positive difference in the lives of those you serve.

Made in United States
Troutdale, OR
12/29/2024

27385709R00066